INVITATION
TO MODERN SKIING

by Fred Iselin and A.C. Spectorsky

WITH ACTION PHOTOGRAPHS BY JOHN O'REAR

AND DRAWINGS BY S. FLEISHMAN

A FIRESIDE BOOK
PUBLISHED BY SIMON AND SCHUSTER

A FIRESIDE BOOK
PUBLISHED BY SIMON AND SCHUSTER
ROCKEFELLER CENTER, 630 FIFTH AVENUE
NEW YORK, NEW YORK 10020

THIRD FIRESIDE PRINTING
SBN 671-21046-7 FIRESIDE PAPERBACK EDITION
LIBRARY OF CONGRESS CATALOG CARD NUMBER: 65-24278
MANUFACTURED IN THE UNITED STATES OF AMERICA

INVITATION TO MODERN SKIING

CONTENTS

INTRODUCTION

The purpose of this book is to teach you to ski for fun, with grace and ease, and always under control, able to stop when you want to, turn away from obstacles, reduce or increase speed at will. This is the art of skiing; it has greater thrills and exhilaration than any other sport known to man. And it is not hard to learn. When you consider that the average novice in skiing is able to devote only about twenty days to the sport in one season, and those days often not consecutively, but in two-day weekends, it becomes apparent that the acquiring of reasonable skill, which is often achieved in the first season, puts skiing in the forefront of sports relatively easy to learn. Yet one can devote an entire lifetime (and a happy one!) to developing and improving, to learning refinements and achieving grace. None of the learning process need be drudgery, either, if a sensible, intelligently worked out and tested system is pursued.

Another misconception about skiing is that one must be young and strong to enjoy it. Yet people in their forties and fifties have taken up the sport for the first time—and are still enjoying it at sixty and over. They are not and they never will be winners of ski-jump and racing competitions, but at all the snow resorts of the world you can see them skimming down slopes in easy, sweeping turns.

There are three ways to learn to ski. One is to get on skis and ride. You may develop balance and a certain amount of zip and speed this way, but you're just as likely to end up in the hospital. Even if you don't, you'll be a constant hazard to yourself and to other skiers. You'll compare with real skiers as a man who can go fast in one direction on skates compares with a figure skater cutting beautiful patterns on the ice to the admiration of all who look on.

The second way to learn to ski is any one of a number of quick, easy shortcuts which offer to teach you without any trouble in a miraculously short time. If you learn that way, you'll be able to perform creditably on slopes of the "correct" gradient, on snow packed just right and of a certain consistency, and, preferably, on the slope on which you received your instruction. But nothing will help you when you find yourself in real skiing country with an interesting variety of terrain and snow conditions; you'll start to turn in your usual way and, to your surprise, you'll keep going straight—if you're lucky. More likely, you will finish the hill on your face, a method of skiing which, experience teaches, is neither pleasant nor elegant.

The third way is the right way: Select a recognized and reputable system of skiing founded on a sound knowledge of the skier's art and follow it diligently, through a logical, step-by-step method of instruction. Experience has shown that this is actually the quickest way to become a real skier. And, incidentally, avail yourself of as much on-the-snow instruction from qualified teachers as it is in your power to obtain.

But right at this point, before we go out onto the slope, so to speak, it is time to stand back from the sport of skiing and look objectively at a unique situation which exists in this sport alone. In our estimation, it is not only unique, it would be uniquely undesirable for any sport. We refer to the fact that, although skiing has grown enormously all over the world since the first edition of this book was published, it has failed to become homogenized and stabilized. We are not suggesting that skiing should become a formalized, closed-end activity (like falconry, for example) because part of its vitality and excitement arises from the fact that it is continuously evolving and improving. But we still deplore the chauvinism and faddism—and resultant confusion for the beginner—that seems to plague skiing, so that there are American ski schools and Austrian ski schools and French ski schools and Swiss ski schools, and splinter groups within them, all with seasonal ups and downs of popularity. One would be hard put to find such unjustified instabilities of methods and procedures in any other sport: there is a right way to play golf, to play tennis, to swim, etc. And the sad fact is that there are many hapless amateurs who can testify that they never got very far in any of these sports because they failed to learn the right way to participate in them. But skiing has been cursed with more than a dozen "right way" methods of instruction. And we must stress that word "instruction" because expert skiers, when they are skiing recreationally and for the sheer joy of it, will all ski pretty much alike, especially when the going gets a bit rough. It is our assertion that the function of any method of instruction is to produce happy and skillful recreational skiers, and that any single phase of the instruction which does not lead directly to this end is unserviceable.

It is our belief that the step-by-step instruction in this book fulfills these desiderata: nothing learned will be discarded; no action or maneuver is presented out of logical learning order; every maneuver proceeds out of the one immediately before it; the most advanced maneuver is the logical culmination of the learning process; the ultimate achievement sought for is the attainment of versatility, grace, mastery—and fun. And we do want to stress the fun part of skiing: among the aspects of the sport which we view with rueful displeasure are the grim determination and brute force that beginners and even intermediate skiers bring to the slope. This is odd; for the best kind of amateur, recreational skiing is noncompetitive. It is not a team sport, it is not even a man-against-man sport, like tennis. Nor is it a sport which might be characterized as man-against-nature. It is—more than any other sport we can think of—man with nature; it is a form of play that has much more in common with the discothèque than the gridiron. It is this kind of joyful and delightful activity that we believe to be the true goal of 99 and 44/100 per cent of all skiers. And it is toward this end that we have shaped this book.

Let's remember, though, that the fun of skiing has its unhappy opposite, typified by the limited skier who has learned one or possibly two flashy maneuvers on one kind of packed slope, who then finds himself floundering in powder snow or thrown by moguls. This may seem ludicrous, but it is a real tragedy to the victim of misteaching, not woefully cynical misteaching, but the kind of misguided teaching that gives both pupil and instructor a feeling of fast accomplishment which is bought at the cost of attaining well-rounded excellence.

The purpose of this book is to spare you such unhappiness. There is only one kind of good skiing: the kind that enables you to cope with whatever conditions may be encountered. Even if you use this book to learn skiing on packed slopes, you will be capable of dealing with deep, rough terrain, bumps and untracked snow when you meet them. It is easier to ski on the packed slope, and it is a temptation to learn a short-cut type of skiing for use on it, but he who learns correctly will be amply repaid on all slopes.

One word of caution, which cannot be too strongly emphasized: If you are a beginner, stick to one reputable, recognized school of instruction. If it is Austrian or American, stick to that. If it is Swiss or French, stick to that. Confusion, misery, and defeat are the lot of the bewildered beginner lost in a maze of systems. All systems have as their goal controlled, easy skiing; their major differences lie in the manner in which they approach their common aim.

It is our contention, however, that the current practice of designating slightly differing techniques by the names of their country of origin is misleading. Part of the reason for this practice has to do with the history of skiing in America, one of whose major characteristics is the importation of foreign ski instructors—often recruited (for their publicity value) from among the ranks of international skiing competition winners. Indubitably, too, the country that wins most competitions in any given year has quite possibly added an improvement or a refinement to competitive skiing. We stress the word "competitive" because very few of these innovations (if any) are meaningful for the teaching or enjoyment of recreational skiing. As we see it, chauvinism, misplaced patriotism, and the glamour of European skiing champions have combined to create an unfortunate misunderstanding. The facts are clear from observation, and they dispel this undesirable myth. The facts are that good and fluent and expert skiing in the correct and modern way is now international. It is this fundamentally correct, modern and international method of skiing and ski instruction that this book is all about.

We have no intention of detracting from any system of instruction. Fine and able teachers of all recognized schools can point with pride to pupils who place high in competitive skiing. We do believe that the system presented in this book is the surest, simplest, most logical, and most easily understood method so far developed. It is a joy to the teacher to see how the pupil unconsciously and automatically brings into play in advanced work the essential elements learned on his first day on the practice slope. You can go from novice to expert by a blended progression which is as smooth and pleasurable as the polished ski runs you can soon be making.

Why Form?

Technique, form, is the mark of the expert, whether he be golfer, pianist, boxer, or skier. Why is this? Because form is the execution of any physical activity with maximum efficiency and minimum effort. We find good form beautiful, aesthetically satisfying, because it is functional and therefore graceful. Physical grace is the handmaid of physical efficiency. The back-swing and follow-through which characterize the drive of the championship tennis player and golfer can be seen, on a smaller scale, in the hand movements of the concert pianist and in the shoulder movements of the great skier. Form—that is, good technique—is not an added quality it would be nice to acquire while becoming a skier; it is an integral part of the sport, of any sport. And it pays amazing dividends.

In skiing, the most advanced and most respected and admired maneuvers are the easiest to do in terms of muscular effort. They are the ultimate in technique, and therefore the ultimate in efficiency. For the same reason, they are beautiful to see. Every exercise, movement, and maneuver in this book will lead you to them gradually. Every link in the learning chain will play its part in the final perfection of your form. We urge you not to skip the seemingly unimportant earlier exercises necessary to mastery. They will make of you a skier whose form is impeccable, whose skiing will light the eyes of the beholder, and fill you with a joy and excitement impossible to describe. You will experience the true thrill of the sport: you, alone, on your skis, at the top of a snow-clad mountain, looking out over distant ranges, then looking down at a steep run, a grove of trees to be threaded, a winding trail, a massive rock formation to be circled, whatever the terrain offers—and knowing you are the master of it. That's skiing!

Retrospect and Prediction

Earlier we talked briefly about the varieties of schools of skiing and the changes within the sport. We'll have a great deal more to say about that and other allied matters in the last chapter of this book— "Final

Thoughts on Schools of Skiing and the Dynamics of the Art." But let's pause here, before we shove off for our first sally on the slopes, to do as all good skiers should before they start a run; let's look behind us and ahead of us to see what we can learn from our vantage point.

Looking back from the perspective of the mid-1960's (and, in Iselin's case, to skiing, literally, all over the world since the last edition of this book was written) one of the most striking things we notice is the speed with which certain names and words in skiing become either dirty words or obsolete words. You will notice that the normal progression is from dirty to obsolete, though we won't propose that this transition is the reason for skiing being described as a clean sport. Arlberg is a dirty word, rapidly becoming clean but obsolete. Tempo turn skipped being a dirty word and just became obsolete. Rotation is now a dirty word, which is a shame, since it is extremely useful and the act itself is virtually as much a part of skiing as ever, though in a somewhat modified form, as we shall see. The words "vorlage" and "rücklage" are as obsolete as maple skis, balloon ski pants, and Great Aunt Edna's wedding gown. The word "swing" has somewhat fallen out of favor and usage, though it is not yet a dirty word. We rather like it: we find it expressive and it has about it just the right amount of connotative connection with the kind of jazz that's fun to dance to, as opposed to the kind that people just sit glumly and listen to, cool and motionless. "Counter-rotation" is a very dirty word these days. When you see expert skiers employing it, you are supposed to look away, as though you were embarrassed. But they do indeed use it. "Wedeln" is not as bright and shiny new as it was a few years ago, but it is still a very clean word. We will go along with that, but we would like to suggest that the skier bear in mind that it is properly a maneuver *in skiing and not a way of skiing to the exclusion of all others. We could go on, but we think you get the idea. Terms in skiing, like schools of skiing, come and go. We are all for this when it spells progress. It is our observation that the operative distinction one must bear in mind is the difference between evolution and revolution: the revolutions have made their contributions, to be sure, but they have not survived. (It is interesting to note that some of the revolutions have been brought on unwittingly by championship slalom and downhill racers, who have developed highly individual styles suited to their physiques and to the exigencies of competition, and have thus, almost by accident, been the recipients of slavish imitation by recreational skiers for whom the style and its uses are largely inapplicable.)*

Meanwhile, skiing continues to flourish with matchless vigor. It is a tribute to the sport that it is able to do so in the light of such wild oscillations of popular fancy in methodology and words used to describe it. With dirty words becoming clean, clean words becoming obsolete, dirty words becoming obsolete and clean, and with pole *length and ski length having their ups and downs almost as rapidly as women's hemlines, it's gratifying to see so many people skiing so well—not to mention at all. Of course, there are dropouts—usually disappointed skiers who have become discouraged by lack of progress. Or by other confusion. Can you imagine the games of tennis or golf, if tennis rackets and golf clubs changed style and pattern every year, and methods of play did, too? Staying with the tennis and golf analogies for a moment: can you imagine trying to play a good game of tennis equipped solely with knowledge of a deep-court volley, or a chop or smash of the sort employed when it's your turn to go up to the net in a game of doubles; or, in the case of golf, can you imagine trying to play eighteen holes without knowing how to do anything but putt, or chip? We don't want to belabor the point, but we don't think it can be given too much importance.*

But skiing does change, and the change brings improvements. Refinements are added, tested, survive, or fall by the wayside. New records are broken in every sport every year, and skiing is no exception. Equipment definitely has improved immensely. Safety bindings alone account for a great deal of improvement in the sport itself: the security they breed permits the emergence of the natural courage that goes with skiing—as opposed to the reckless death-wish kind of courage that produces more broken bones than broken records. Other factors have contributed to the amazing growth of the sport: rapid and inexpensive travel, the opening of new areas all over the world, man-made snow on slopes near urban areas, even such peripheral factors as the comfort and elegance and sex appeal of ski wear—all have added their bit to the growth of the sport.

And now we will indulge in that promised bit of prediction. We can already see the signs of a gradual amalgamation of all schools of skiing. We applaud variety, but we feel that too much of it can be not only distracting and confusing, but also destructive. It is neither our hope nor our prediction that everyone will teach the same, learn the same, ski the same. This would be a drag—but there is nothing to worry about because the very nature of skiing and individual differences of skiers and terrain thankfully preclude drab sameness. But we do think the sport is steadying down and beginning to grow into a cohesive whole. One of our main reasons for thinking thus may be gleaned from a passing remark made earlier, when we pointed out that the experts from all schools of skiing tend to ski much the same when doing so for the sheer pleasure of it, or when conditions are difficult. And there is a good reason for this. As we have said, a distinguishing characteristic of the true expert is his versatility. Specialists win races, versatile skiers win friends and influence people—and have a hell of a lot of fun doing it. If we may risk your boredom with one more analogy: the recreational horseback rider does not stand up in his short stirrups and lean out over the horse's neck; nor, for that matter, does the fox hunter in the field attempt to take his horse over gates and fences while mounted in a Western roping saddle. These are truisms; everyone takes them for granted. We predict that the same kind of good sense is going to continue to gain ground in skiing so that (to pursue the analogy) the accomplished skier will be able to make use of all that is available to him in the art, just as the accomplished rider learns some of his skills from each of the specialized disciplines of his sport.

One final prediction—and a word of explanation. We confidently predict that any man or woman of normal physical endowment can learn to become a versatile and happy skier by following the procedures described in this book. But we wish to repeat and to stress that one does not become a skier by reading about it. Most people learn a great deal from observation, without quite realizing it. Certainly on-the-slope instruction is far more valuable than reading a description of it. But it is our assertion that the detailed analyses provided here not only constitute guidance for those who want to understand what they are doing, but also for those who recognize the importance of understanding what they are doing wrong, and who are determined to learn how to do things right. In the last analysis, the best analysis is self-analysis. Rapidity in learning—in achieving the kind of mastery the expert skier enjoys—is measured less by physical endowment than by guided practice along a preplanned route toward the ultimate goal. We believe this book provides that guidance and that preplanning. And we wish you good skiing.

CHAPTER ONE

PRELIMINARIES

How to Use This Book

Three things are essential to learning the art of skiing correctly: practice, patience, understanding.

The practice may be hard to come by; not all of us can ski as much as we would like to, and the weekend skier is too often tempted to extract what fun he can with the little he knows, rather than devoting a modicum of his time to improving his technique in the belief that this promises far greater fun to come. Such people, and those who have gone through the so-called short-cut courses of instruction, are what we call "stopped skiers"; that is, they have progressed to a certain degree and there they stay. Practice in skiing pays dividends fast, in progress and enjoyment. *So, follow the instructions in this book carefully, and don't go beyond any step until you have fully mastered it.* Even then, a half-hour warmup on each skiing day, in which you rapidly and skillfully go through some elementary maneuvers again, is extremely valuable. Even concert pianists warm up by playing scales and velocity exercises.

Patience is a virtue which no one can teach you. But remember this: It is in the five minutes *after* you feel like giving up that things suddenly come right and you do with ease what seemed beyond your ability to learn.

Understanding the principles, dynamics, movements (and reasons for them) in all the skiing maneuvers is necessary to their learning and correct execution. Read the explanations step by step; consult the diagrams often; as you read in your room, stand up and "sense" the movements described.

If you feel you want to, you can skip the chapters on equipment, a typical downhill run, competitive skiing, and several other parts of the book which are not absolutely essential. But don't gloss over or skip the earlier chapters for the later, more spectacular ones, even if you consider yourself something of a skier already. If you do, you may become a "stopped skier."

A word about the photographs in this book. If you want flashy action shots with a plume of powder snow and a skier whizzing down a seemingly perpendicular slope, go to your travel agent or a newsreel theater. The pictures included here are chosen for their clarity. Study the position of feet, skis, body, knees, shoulders, arms, and head. Look at the pictures marked "wrong," as well as those marked "right." The most typical faults of beginners are shown. Are you guilty of them? If so, you will find the cause and cure in the text.

And do not ignore the do's and don'ts at the end of each chapter. They represent a synthesis of many years of experience in teaching all kinds of pupils, from rank amateur to near-expert, and include not only a recapitulation of important points explained in the text but also additional "ounces of prevention" to keep you from falling into errors which would prove hard to cure.

And now, you're off on your way to mastery of the world's most thrilling and inspiring sport. Work hard at it—and good skiing!

Equipment

There are dry-run skiers, just as there are dry-run sailors, fishermen, amateur photographers. These are usually gadget-happy types who are more interested in the gear of the sport than in the sport itself. Usually, these "experts" are full of advice on what is the latest and best in equipment; usually, they are constantly adding to their gear and rejecting last year's favorite acquisitions. You can't become a sportsman by buying, but these characters try to do so and are constantly disappointed at their failure, which they blame on their guiltless purchases. In recent years, the development of many kinds and types of ski equipment has made ski-gear buying a full-time occupation for the dry-run folk. We give them this much space here so you'll recognize them when you see them. That's important if you're new to skiing and are out to equip yourself—learn to spot the so-called expert and run away from him just as fast as you can. He can talk you into spending too much money, into buying dubious gadgetry, and into thinking it costs hundreds of dollars to get equipped for a snow-bunny weekend. Not so, not so—as we shall see.

Skiing need not be an expensive sport. Wisely purchased equipment, selected for excellence of materials and workmanship rather than for looks alone (though let's face it, good-looking gear gives a lift to the spirits—and to après ski conquests), is now widely available and, given proper care, will last many seasons and in most cases many years. Bearing this in mind, don't practice false economy. The difference between a thirty-dollar pair of adequate boots and a fifty-dollar pair of better boots, prorated over say five years, is just four dollars a year; the difference between the two in happy skiing may be immeasurable.

And don't get buyer's fever; take your time, shop, compare, think over a purchase before you make it. Increasingly, equipment is available for rent at the ski slopes. We do not recommend relying on rental; equipment used and misused by others is never as satisfactory as that which you own; but rental can offer you an opportunity to try out equipment about which you may be in doubt. The rapid growth of skiing has been accompanied by a proliferation of equipment, not all of it good. If you're in doubt about any of it which you're considering buying, a rental pre-purchase trial may help you to decide.

Here is the recommended order in which to spend your money and invest your best judgment when buying ski gear: Do not stint on boots and bindings. They are the most important part of your outfit, since an absolutely firm juncture of boot and ski is essential, and since every foot and body movement must be transmitted to the ski. Skis and poles come next, then ski pants, underwear, socks, gloves or mittens, sweaters, knapsack; various trimmings of real or fancied usefulness come last.

BOOTS

Ski boots are of many types (some of which are shown on the facing page) but they must all measure up to the same set of qualifications if they are going to do their job well. A good ski boot has a thick sole (usually steel-shanked) and uppers of stout yet pliable leather. Boots must fit snugly. If they are too tight, they will be useless and they'll virtually guarantee cold feet, but if they fit loosely, they will not afford the kind of control required in skiing, where every movement of the foot must be communicated to the ski without lost motion inside an ill-fitting boot.

When buying boots, take along your own ski socks and ski pants which go down into the boot. Stores supply socks for trying on boots, but your own socks are necessary for you to be certain of correct fit. Put on a pair of lightweight wool socks and over them a pair of heavy, raw-wool, outer socks. Grasp the tips of both socks together and pull them free of your toes, so that the inside sock will not cramp the foot. Try to ease your foot into the new boot without letting the friction pull the toes of the socks up tight. Before lacing the boot, kick the heel against the door so that the foot is well back against the heel of the boot.

Now lace the boot firmly, keeping the tongue or inner boot unwrinkled and straight. The laced edges of the uppers should not close or come closer than a finger's width to each other; if they do, the uppers may stretch enough to prevent a sufficiently tight lacing. If the laced edges are too far apart, snow may penetrate the boot, and the laces won't give you the firmness and support required over the instep.

With the boot laced up, stand squarely on the floor and try to wriggle your toes. They should not feel cramped, but they must not have free play inside the boot. A snug, comfortable fit is desirable. Now start to rise on your toes. Your heel should not come up off the sole of the boot. Now bend your knees and lean forward from the ankles, keeping your heels on the floor. The boot top should not cut into the front of your ankle.

If the boot is all right in the above respects, and if it is made by a

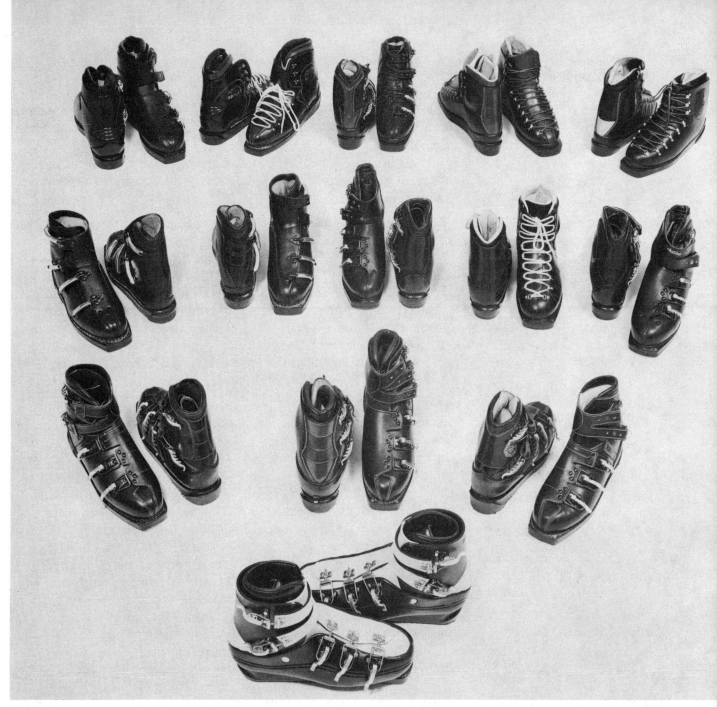

BOOTS. Most all well-made ski boots today feature good support, good padding, easier closure via racing-hook lacing or buckles, and inner boot for additional snugness and firmness without cramping or cutting off circulation. Here is a representative selection. TOP ROW, LEFT TO RIGHT: Koflach Gold Star for men, accordian-hinged, molded tongue, lace inner boot, buckle outer boot; Koflach Snow Star for men and women, double laced, foam padded, hinged and tapered heel; Reiker Sealed Sole for men and women, reinforced ankle support, five-buckle adjustable closure; Reiker Sealed Sole for men, speed lacing on inner boot, racing hooks on outer boot; Reiker Sealed Sole for men or women of intermediate skill has hinged heel and pulled-through racing hooks. SECOND ROW, LEFT TO RIGHT: Garmisch boot with four adjustable Raichle buckles; Garmisch with five Raichle buckles offering finer ad-justment; Nordica Meteor, featuring narrower fitted heel and concealed storm welting; Nordica Sestriere, an excellent boot for men or women recreational skiers, at a modest price; Nordica Meteor Racer is what the name implies, but is also suitable for recreational ski-ing. THIRD ROW, LEFT TO RIGHT: Henke Speedfit Rocket for men and women, an excellent all-around boot with five-buckle closure, molded sponge padding, silicone-treated leather construction; Henke Speedfit Racer, an expert's boot with extreme stiffness of shell, six buckles for exact fit; Henke Speedfit Downhill for men and women, an extremely sturdy boot for heavy use, with five-buckle closure and extra reinforcement. BOTTOM: the PK/Lange Custom-Fit Plastic Boot has outer plastic boot and inner boot of epoxy-fiberglass, five-buckle closure.

reliable craftsman, you can now pay attention to its cosmetic aspects, but don't let looks influence you before the boot proves itself functionally.

There are over a hundred makes and types of ski boot on the market today. Most of the good modern boots have the following four features in their favor:

1. Availability in various widths and lasts, as well as in length sizes, thus assuring you of correct fit.
2. An inner boot, pliable and often padded, which can give the ankle good support without constricting the entire foot.
3. Comparative lightness. A sturdy boot need not be a clumsy one; steel shank in the sole and good leather with lightweight padding combine to make a boot which won't retard climbing or make you look like a deep-sea diver.
4. Soft enough leather in the uppers so that boot can lace fairly high yet not inhibit bending at ankles.

What should a boot cost? It depends on your finances and the kind of skiing you do. For the occasional-weekend skier, about $30 should be adequate. For the average recreational skier who gets out more often, and for longer periods, $40 to $50 should do it nicely. Experts and competition skiers will not be likely to be seeking advice here; however, should you wish to equip yourself with boots as they do, $60 up will do the trick—and may your skiing be as good as your boots!

Says Spectorsky: "As an occasional skier lo these many years, I like the fact that the new, better boots don't require too much breaking in. The foam or sponge padding aids a lot in comfort and support for the feet of the normally sedentary. As a man with a long foot, I'm delighted by the narrower soles of the newer boots, which don't overlap the sides of the skis the way the older, wider soles did."

Says Iselin: "Out on the slopes all day, standing while teaching and skiing day after day, I've had plenty of opportunity to evaluate the newer boots. They are definitely superior to what was available ten years or more ago. I've also seen every degree of amateur skier and have talked to dozens of competition skiers, teachers, coaches, Olympic skiers all over the world. In discussing recommendations with my co-author, we decided it would be better to name names—and risk hurt feelings about unfair omissions—than to withhold the fruits of experience."

Well, then. The major bootmakers have various styles and models, with new models appearing virtually every year. Those bearing the following names are deemed especially worthy of your consideration: Haderer, Strolz, Rogg, and Henke for the expert and for downhill and slalom; Garmisch and Nordica for a somewhat less costly boot. Other excellent boots include Strasser, Kastinger, Humanic, Raichle, Rieker, Molitor, Bass, Le Trappeur, Dolomite, Sandler. This is not an exhaustive list by far, but it's a fine starter; chances are you'll find fit and price to suit you and your skiing among the boots bearing these names.

Boot development is not standing still, however, and if you have the time, the pelf, and the inclination, you might want to try some of the innovations, among the best of which is the buckle closure first developed by Henke. These boots close with clamps (somewhat like the old galoshes) and most have a self-closing inner boot; even with a gloved hand you can loosen these boots while resting or riding a lift, then snap them tight in a jiffy. Another innovation: uppers cut and stitched in two separate parts, to permit a hinge action for extreme forward leg action.

As we said, in buying boots—as well as all equipment—take your time. Be sure of fit, be sure of adequate support, don't go by looks. Finally, don't expect your boots to be completely waterproof; they should be snowproof, but if they were waterproof your feet would perspire and the perspiration might freeze. The result is not fun. It is hard to ski with a few toes missing.

BINDINGS

The function of the ski binding is to hold the boots rigidly to the skis. Just as it is up to the boot to hold the foot firmly enough to reflect every motion of the body (transmitted through legs and feet) to the binding, so the binding must continue this transmission of forces to the ski. A wobbly, infirm binding, with play in it, defeats controlled skiing.

A decade ago, the lethal aspects of the rigid binding were accepted as one of the hazards of the sport. Torques and strains resulting from spills pitted the whole leverage of the ski against human bone and sinew with predictably painful results. The binding held the skier to the lever and it was the skier's anatomy that lost the unequal struggle. There were, to be sure, a few safety devices designed to release the grip of the binding on the boot under too great stress, but they were at best tricky, intricate and unreliable; at worst, they popped open in mid-turn while the skier was "swinging," or they failed altogether in their function of holding the boot rigidly to the ski.

Then a major revolution took place. Inventive gadgeteers, spurred by the growth of the sport and the emphasis on high-speed downhill skiing (and the increase in fractures), set to work to perfect a binding which would hold as effectively as any non-safety binding ever devised, but which would release its grip before endangering its wearer.

It would be foolish to predict that no further improvement in bindings will be forthcoming. But it can be said with certainy that the best modern safety bindings do their jobs superbly. And they have won a psychological as well as a physical victory. When they first made their appearances on the slopes, the experts ignored them and the show-off hot shots sneered at them as sissy stuff, comparable to water

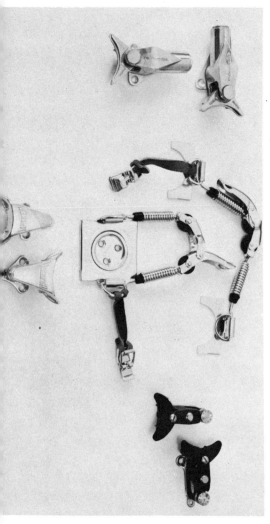

SEPARATE COMPONENTS. LEFT: A pair of Marker Automatic-Simplex toe irons. RIGHT, TOP TO BOTTOM: Nevada adjustable toe irons, Marker LDR longthong turntable and roller-lever cables, Ski Free Super Deluxe toe irons (suitable for competition skiing).

wings for swimmers, fit only for beginners. Now every skier with common sense and the desire to keep skiing uses nothing else. Even in the toughest competition skiing, the safety binding is used virtually exclusively. And speaking of psychology—what greater tonic for the beginner's mental attitude could there be than the feeling of security to be derived from safety bindings?

But this brings us to an urgent note of warning. The safety binding *must* be affixed to the ski, and adjusted to the skier's boots, by a qualified expert. Its release point—the setting of its safety action—must be regulated by an expert. Learn from him how to adjust it and check it, then do so frequently. Otherwise, your serene sense of security may be shattered most rudely by the sound of a bone cracking!

Are safety bindings really safe? Consider this statistic: In a recent season at a Western resort known for its steep runs, out of twenty-six thousand pupils there were only ten who suffered fractures; of those who suffered them, *six wore non-safety bindings*. Automobile driving should be as safe!

A couple of paragraphs back, we warned about the necessity for correct mounting and adjustment of safety bindings. This *is* important, but one should not be misled into thinking these bindings are complex or fragile, or that they require constant tinkering. It's only good sense to check all your gear before you take off, anyway. Learn how to check the adjustment of your bindings, and they'll give you rugged and dependable service, plus that confidence which is so important to rapid progress. Incidentally, don't get the impression that the more expert you get, the stiffer the release mechanism will be, or should be, set. If you ski technically correctly, the binding can be set very loose, even for high-speed skiing.

Safety bindings are of two major types: heel tight and heel free. Both do their jobs and there is much controversy over which is the better. Far be it from us to take sides; a pretty good guide to the kind you should select is to observe which is favored by the better skiers and the instructors in the terrain where you'll do most of your skiing, because the chances are that terrain and kind of skiing have influenced the relative popularity of the two kinds of bindings. In either case, the release of heel or toe frees the entire boot. One governing consideration: If you plan to do any touring, or much walking about on your skis, you'll probably select a heel-free binding. Either style is suitable for all snow conditions. For a selection of excellent safety bindings, see photographs at left and right.

A final caveat before we get to actual makes of bindings: A released ski will run away from you unless it's tethered to your boot in some way; a long strap is not recommended (although these are sold) because in a bad fall the ski may windmill around the skier and cut or gouge him. We advocate the Arlberg Safety strap, or one similar to it.

Many experts and instructors who have experimented with safety bindings have found they prefer to create their own combinations of heel and toe devices. We see no reason why the amateur and beginner should not profit from this, and our recommendations, which follow, indicate such combinations when they're deemed desirable. Once more apologizing for omissions, we list our choices here, with a few comments on each.

A fine choice for all-round skiing is the new Marker Simplex toe release unit, used with Snaplock heel release cable; or the Nevada toe unit combined with Look Grand Prix heel release. If you don't like a rigid, inflexible heel release, use the Lift cable, or the Attenhofer Safety Flex, Dovre or Kandahar safety cables. For complete bindings, we recommend such makes as Dovre and Kandahar.

If you plan no touring on your ski trips, an excellent binding is the Marker Swivel Longthong. An alternative, with similar design, is the Anderson & Thompson. Both do a fine job of providing safety while holding the heel down firmly to the skis, essential in modern, high-speed skiing. These bindings can even be used for jumping, a particularly grueling test of their strength and design.

For the recreational skier, the Cubco provides a simple, easily adjusted mechanism with a positive release. Its unsuitability for touring is the only thing which keeps it from being designated all-purpose.

For economy and good design, we suggest the Ski Free combined with Attenhofer Safety Flex cable, a combination which is hard to beat for virtually any condition of skiing or degree of skier's skill.

The Tyrolia is an excellent binding for all forms of skiing, including touring, as is the Dovre, which operates on much the same design principle. Their versatility is bought at the expense of simplicity; adjustment is not quite so easy as with some others, but it is readily learned—and worth it.

There are some dozen or more other bindings available which do their work excellently; the foregoing were named to provide guidance, not to discriminate against all others.

Your bindings, like your boots, can last a long time and can "graduate" from one pair of skis to another. Bindings range in price from about $20 up.

COMPLETE BINDINGS. LEFT TO RIGHT: the Tyrolia Junior; the Tyrolia 800 with adjustable Strammer throw, toe-free unit and flexible heel cable; the popular and simple Cubco.

SKIS

In the technological revolution which has so radically affected ski gear in the past dozen years, the evolution of the skis themselves is as remarkable as the development of the safety binding. Twenty years ago, the industry standard and the preferred ski of the experts was solid hickory. Cheaper skis (then considered adequate for the beginner) were made of maple and ash. Although skis with steel edges were worn by most skiers, especially on packed slopes, and by all experts, almost half the skis sold relied on the wood itself for bite and control in turns, or had the edges mounted after purchase.* In those days, when the authors were at work on the manuscript of the first *Invitation to Skiing*, we were testing on the slopes at Sun Valley a variety of "new" skis—laminates, metal, combination metal and wood, etc.—but at that time the hickory ski was still deemed the best and most reliable.

All this is changed. The skier's concern about matched skis of equal camber (the bowed springiness of the skis), about straight grain, about the dangers of warping and twisting, about the right kind of press to retain ski shape, is no more. *All* the features which used to distinguish a good ski are still desirable; there has been no change in aim or in basic functional design; but they can all be had now in skis which are uniformly excellent, retain their shape and camber, do not vary from ski to ski or from pair to pair, and can be depended upon to serve with a minimum of care and upkeep. Today, when you set out to buy a pair of skis, you can feel confident that lemons are rare, and that most of the better-known makes of moderately priced skis (on up) will be superior in performance and durability to the best that was available even a decade ago. Today's preferred materials are plastic and metal laminates, epoxy, fiberglass.

But how to select your skis from the bewildering variety that you are offered? It's a tough question, to which two don'ts may prove better guides than any positive advice. First—and we concede we're beginning to sound like a broken record—don't select your skis by looks. Skis come in as many colors as cars—including two-tone and three-tone. If you like color, let it be the last consideration in your purchase. Next, beware of fads. Skiers—on the whole an independent and clear-sighted fraternity—are sheeplike in this respect. Whenever a championship is won on a particular make of ski its sales soar, as though the inanimate ski were a magic talisman for assuring good skiing. Then another champion comes along, with different skis, and last year's favorite becomes this year's also-ran. Certainly the ski selections of winning competition skiers are a legitimate guide to excellence; just as surely, last year's winning skis—and next year's—are as good as this year's, especially for the noncompetitive skier.

---

* This is extraordinary, for steel edges were used in slalom competition in 1926 at Davos. In a field of some eighty skiers, the Lantschner brothers, from Innsbruck, proved unbeatable. Later it was discovered that a man named Lettner had secretly installed the clumsy prototypes of today's Lettner edge (which consists of interlocking short sections) on the Lantschners' skis, and a great howl of foul play went up from the other competitors; but the jury ruled in favor of the brothers, and the edge became standard in competition very quickly. Lettner had neglected to patent his edges, and imitations and modifications were and are numerous. Interlocking edges, one-piece edges, side-mounted, flush-mounted, angle-mounted, offset-mounted—all had their innings and still do. In the gabfests of ski lodges all over the world, experts fight the battle of the edge year round. The amateur's best bet is to entrust the choice of edge to the manufacturer of his ski—a wise course if for no other reason than that skis come equipped with these edges anyway.

Once certain that you are in a reputable shop where only excellent merchandise is carried, the suitability of a pair of skis to *you* is of greater importance than the brand name it carries. But since all the best brands come in a variety of lengths and stiffnesses (the two principal considerations in selecting the right skis for you), we recommend restricting your shopping to the better-known, use-tested-by-experts brands. Some of the finest are pictured on page 26.

Length is the first consideration in buying skis, once you've satisfied yourself about quality. The drawing at the right shows the correct way to measure skis. Standing normally erect, raise the arm comfortably; the ski, with its heel on the floor and held vertically, should have its tip reach the palm. Currently there is something of a fad for short skis, and novices sometimes make the mistake of thinking shorter skis will be easier to maneuver, a belief which is fostered by their initial difficulty with the kick turn. Don't be misled; too short skis are less stable than the proper length and will be unequal to the demands of the dynamics of turning, sideslipping, and stopping. Alternatively, skis which are too long will be hard to control, especially in tight turns. The beginner may find a slightly short ski somewhat easier to learn on; if you're buying with this in mind, select the length which reaches to the base of the thumb—no shorter.

When you hold a pair of skis with their running surfaces together, you will note that the heels and the start of the upturn at the tips touch, and that the rest of the skis curve out from each other, with the greatest separation at the point where the platforms for the ski bindings are located. This curvature is called "camber" and is designed so that when you stand on the skis they will flatten out and distribute your weight along the entire running surfaces of the skis. If the springiness of this camber is too strong for your weight, the heels and tips of the skis will dig into the snow. If the skis are too limber for you, the midsection will sag and bear all your weight. Do not mistake stiffness in the ski for strong camber. Even the springiest skis, for very heavy people, must be flexible. Similarly, do not mistake a soft and lifeless ski for one of light springiness. A ski should feel live and flexible in your hands when you bend it.

The most common error in buying skis is to buy a pair which has too strong a camber, so that the skier's weight does not flatten out the curve and get the whole ski on the snow. It is better to have too little camber than too much. Put both skis on the floor and stand on the platforms where the bindings will go. You should not be able to insert a card or piece of paper under the ski at any point behind the upturn if your skis have too much camber they will dig in at tips and tails, and you will be unable to maneuver.

Unless there's a special reason for it, avoid the purchase of special-purpose skis. Jumping skis, with their great length and triple grooves, have no place on the ski slope. The very light, unedged and narrow

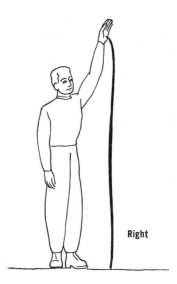

How to Measure Skis

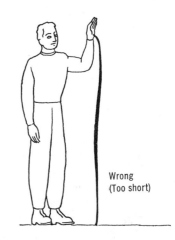

Right

Wrong
(Too short)

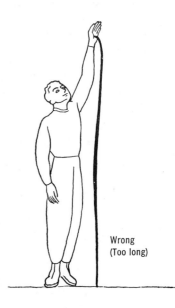

Wrong
(Too long)

SKIS. LEFT TO RIGHT: Blizzard Super Epoxi Fiberglas features sandwich-type glued core with full-length, glued, profiled spring steel edges; Peter Kennedy stainless steel and plastic ski for beginners and intermediates—sides are brushed stainless steel with gunmetal edges formed to protect sides from scuffs and abrasions, polyethylene no-wax base; Kastle Fiberplast Reisenslalom ski, among the finest Austrian epoxi imports; Northland Epoxi-Glass Slalom ski with P-tex bottom features limber tip and stiffer heel profile for holding and tracking ability, interlocking steel edges, epoxi-fiberglass molded top and bottom with laminated hickory and ash core, sides of polyurethene plastic and plastic top finish with inlaid plastic top edges; Yamaha All-Round Epoxi ski of sandwich construction (ash between layers of fiberglass and epoxi resin), high carbon steel hidden edges, stainless tip and tail protectors, polyethylene base; Hart Javelin Combination ski features "L" type welded-on edges and is made of tough stainless alloy with excellent sharpness retention; Head Competition Giant Slalom, a superior ski for racers and other experts, has running surface of high-density polyethylene, a racing base, deep, L-shaped racing-type full-length edges, firm flexibility under foot and heel; Head Standard, ideal for beginners and recreational intermediates, has one-piece edges of tempered steel, inlaid from tip to tail, contoured shape, medium flexibility, construction of metal sandwich with single top-and-bottom plates of tempered, missile-grade aluminum alloy.

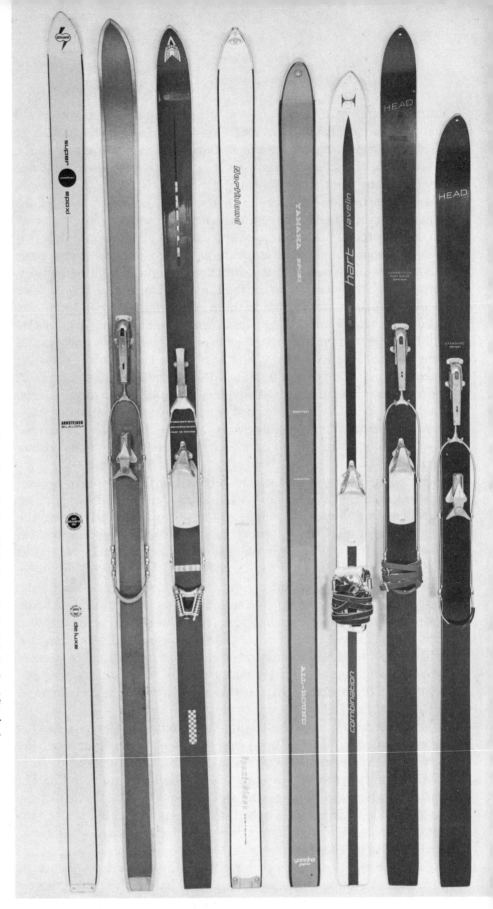

cross-country ski is suitable only for cross-country running. The specialized slalom racer's ski, while it is highly maneuverable, is not too good for all-purpose and recreational skiing. Its offset edges may protrude abnormally far and can trip the recreational skier, and although its soft steel can be (and is) honed to razor sharpness for competition, it loses its keenness quickly and requires constant re-sharpening. Your best bet is the highly maneuverable regular slalom ski, or, perhaps better for beginners and intermediate skiers, the combination downhill and slalom. On the best of these, the steel edges are hard enough to hold their keenness and are sharp enough for fine control, yet they are not so hard as to diminish the ski's natural flexibility. The edge offset is slight. Avoid the specialized downhill ski; it tends to be stiffer and harder to turn. A rough-and-ready rule for determining ski flexibility that's right for you: For girls and smaller men (up to 125 pounds) try the "soft" grade first; men up to 180 pounds should do well with the "medium" grade; heavier men will require a harder grade. Give consideration, too, to the kind of snow conditions you'll be most likely to encounter. The deeper and softer the snow, the more flexible and softer the ski should be, and vice versa. Virtually all skis made these days are sold with a bottom finish already applied.

And now to our specific recommendations—again, with the understanding that this listing is selective and not exhaustive, and that many fine skis are not named.

Irrespective of cost, Head skis may well be considered first choice for American skiing. Developed and manufactured in this country, constantly tested, they are superb precision devices, making use of metal, plastic and wood in a virtually indestructible combination. The Head Standard is recommended for every kind of recreational skiing. Head competition skis are much favored by downhill racers.

Northland is another domestic manufacturer of fine skis, available in a variety of models, from inexpensive on up. Even their most expensive ski is not out of range for the average recreational skier.

Blizzard skis are high rankers in the higher-priced lines, as are those of Kästles, Sohler and Kneissl, especially the Kneissl epoxy skis. The latter are favorites with what may be a majority of racers. These skis feature a very limber forward section and tip, with greater stiffness from the binding back; many experts believe this makes for greater speed, especially in schusses with the weight a bit back.

Rossignol makes a fine metal ski with very fast plastic bottom. Excellent skis are also made by Fischer, Erbacher, Hart, Gresvig, Authier, Rosskopf, and others.

A good pair of skis can be yours for $75 on up, though adequate, less expensive skis are available—as are superb skis costing more than twice as much. Since modern skis are so durable and trouble-free, a largish investment in them is more justified than it would have been years ago when skis required far more frequent replacement than they do today.

POLES

The vogue for short poles is obsolete, and a good thing, too. They were inadequate for balance, timing, climbing, and for use in turning. The vogue for too-long poles is also passed—an equally good thing. This short-lived vogue resulted from the fact that some skiers, observing the success of slalom racers who had abandoned the short pole for a longer one, assumed that you can't have too much of a good thing and began using poles reaching to their shoulders and even higher.

Today, the pendulum swing from too long (back in the twenties) to too short, to too long again is thankfully over. Your correct pole length is measured this way: have the top of the hand grip rest easily a bit under the armpit when the point is on the floor. This will provide you with poles which are long enough to aid you in balance and pole turns, and which will help you attain rhythm and timing.

The preferred all-purpose pole you select will probably be a metal alloy. It is extremely strong, light enough, almost unbreakable (and if it does break, it usually breaks clean), and won't bend as will some aluminum poles. Cane and taped bamboo are enjoying a minor resurgence of popularity, but they have drawbacks which include a tendency to splinter if they break and lesser durability than metal. Glass has proven better for fishing rods than for ski poles.

Grips are very important. They should be sufficiently thick to afford good padding and should not tend to slip from the gloved hand when wet. Plastic may slip in this way; leather is excellent, molded rubber is excellent.

The wrist strap should be amply long for easy accommodation of the gloved hand, wide enough to prevent cutting of the wrist and twisting, and nicely flexible. Some poles have adjustable straps, which may prove handy but are not a compelling consideration.

In examining poles before purchase, satisfy yourself that the attachment of ring to pole is stout and secure. All too often a cheap but gaudy pole, when thrust into the snow for support, keeps right on going down through the snow and into the ground, while the snow ring, broken free of its single cotter pin fastening, rides up the shaft like a monkey on a stick.

Snow rings are available in a variety of materials: plastic, aluminum, rubber, rattan, Duralumin, etc. The Duralumin is probably best, combining lightness with great strength. Rattan is cheapest and least durable.

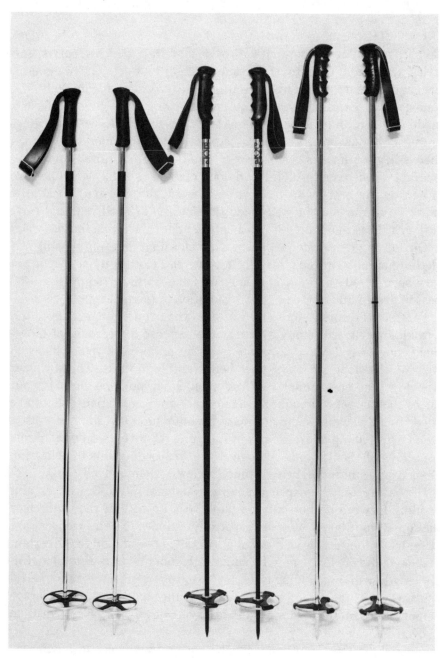

POLES. LEFT TO RIGHT: Head steel poles with black neoprene grips, adjustable leather straps, bantamweight snow rings with vulcanized rubber webbing; PK (Peter Kennedy) ski poles are among the best of the high-strength, lightweight aluminum poles, have fixed straps and notched grips; Scott–U.S.A. deluxe steel poles have rigid steel shafts, finger-notched grips, adjustable straps.

The point of the pole should be good steel but need not be extremely sharp. The photo above shows the desirable details of three excellent makes of poles.

Among alloy poles which test high in use and have excellent straps, grips and other design features, we recommend those made by Northland, Eckel, Scott, Head, Kennedy, Barrecrafters, among others. An adequate pair of poles may be had for as little as $8; excellent poles needn't cost more than $25.

SKI CLOTHING

Ski garb is available in a great variety of materials, designs, colors, and styles. Individual taste must be your guide in its selection. In general, the gaudier gear is worn by the younger, gayer skiers. It's unlikely that a novice can go far wrong in equipment, since even the shoddiest is made by firms having some experience in the field; with clothing, however, it has been known to happen that a clothier who thinks there's a good market for ski wear (and there is) turns out skiing wearables that aren't usables. We don't claim at all that you'll be sure of getting the best by spending a lot—especially if you're hooked by snazzy trimmings—but well-made ski clothing of good material can't cost as little as that which is poorly made or of inferior material.

Obviously, the same applies to all clothing; but purchasing ski clothing entails two hazards all its own: the clothes must perform a very specialized function and look well too—which requires expertness in design and construction (in addition to mere fit).

PANTS.   Trimness and slimness are what you want—a snug and wrinkle-free fit. Don't buy a pair at the expense of freedom of movement, however. Try on ski pants over the underwear you're likely to wear on the slope; do a few knee bends and high kicks. The straps or webbing that pass under the foot should not pull too tightly. Your knees should feel complete freedom of motion. Stretch pants should be tried, by all means; their elasticity permits superbly snug fit with a wonderful feeling of freedom—in fact, one who wears them is hardly conscious of them at all—though if the wearer happens to be a well-shaped girl, others will be very much aware of them indeed.

If you are tall, be especially sure that bending at the knees and bending forward do not pull the pants legs up so that they will clear the top of your boots. Women especially—since women's trousers are often made long in the seat but short in the legs—should make certain that ski pants are long enough (come high enough) in the crotch. Over-all length will not compensate for a too-short inseam and too-low waist. On the other hand, it's safe to get a quite tight waist; the average person of sedentary habits usually loses one or two inches of waistline in even one week of daily skiing.

One of the most common mistakes made by novices in buying ski pants (and ski parkas, too) is to purchase them for warmth. Warmth is supplied by undergarments; ski pants and parkas should be light in weight, closely woven, smooth, and snow repellent.

In purchasing ski pants and parkas, make sure there are plenty of pockets, and that the pockets are provided with zipper or overlapped toggle or large-button closure. Zippers should have a large enough tab to be drawn open or closed without requiring removal of gloves.

UNDERWEAR.   The comfortable skier is he who has next to his buff a full-length suit of armor against the cold. Get it large enough to allow easy movement without binding at arms, shoulders, or crotch, but not so large that it will bunch up. Fifty per cent wool or all-wool, when available, are about equally good. All-wool has a slight edge in this respect but is harder to care for and launder without shrinking. Silk provides excellent warmth since it is lightweight and has little bulk. Red flannel is thought quite gay by some, but unless awareness of it gives you an inner glow, the color won't affect your body temperature. Mesh-woven and two-ply underwear, all or part synthetic, traps air and thus insulates nicely. Skiers should eschew down-filled quilted underwear which is fine for hunters but tends to be a bit bulky for skiing. (Quilted parkas are O.K.)

Socks. You will need two pairs of socks inside your ski boots, a lightweight under pair and a heavier outer pair. A half-size difference between these pairs is advisable. The inner pair should be soft, pure washed wool, but one should avoid the kind of lovely-looking fuzzy wool which rolls up into balls under your feet. The outer pair should be of unwashed wool, the kind of wool that has the natural oils left in, which makes it moisture repellent. When you buy your socks, buy sock stretchers to dry them on after washing. Tight socks and good skiing don't go together. Himalaya stretch socks—specifically designed for skiing—are excellent.

Gloves. Cold hands are the bane of the winter sportsman, but they need not be if the advice of the experts is taken. Ordinary lined gloves are not always satisfactory. The leather wets through all too often, for one thing. For another, fleece- or fur-lined gloves soon get worn, matted down, and thin at the finger tips, which are most vulnerable to cold. And most gloves are either too short in the cuff to make a closure with the jacket sleeve or, if they are the gauntlet type, too flared to keep out snow. Your best bet is to consider only those gloves and gauntlets which are designed for skiing. These will provide warmth, good closure, ample length at wrist, water repellent leather all around or on palms only (with wool back), and a removable or integral lining warm enough and durable enough to give you warmth all day long.

Mittens are not especially recommended. Years ago they were preferred, especially those which came in outer and inner separate mitts, called choppers and liners. There's nothing wrong with good ski mittens and it's true that having all fingers of the hand in contact, and in the same air space as the hand itself, makes keeping the entire hand warm a much surer bet. But this virtue is pretty much offset by the inconvenience of manipulating gear and equipment with the mittens on—and taking them off may mean that they and the bare hand will become too chilled to warm up again in a hurry.

Sweaters. Two lightweight, good-quality sweaters are warmer than one heavy one. Slipovers are preferable to cardigans; round or

SKI AND APRÈS-SKI GARB. CLOCK-WISE: Rib-knit all-wool ski hood that can also roll up into a cap; men's strap-buckled after-ski boots of shearing-lined seal (from Abercrombie & Fitch); Henke men's back-zippered after-ski boots; Patault racing gloves; Olympia ski gloves; Henke fur-trimmed buck after-ski boots and Henke zipper-back seal after-ski boots, both for women. The *pièce de résistance* in center is a suede car coat (by Robert Lewis) lined with white pile; it has a drawstring hood and wolf trim, and an appliquéd skua bird design to be casually revealed when the coat is doffed; on its sleeve are reversible wool headband-ear-warmers and hair-out-of-the-eyes-keepers.

turtleneck sweaters will give more protection to throat and chest than V-neck, but V-necks are fine with lightweight turtleneck shirts underneath.

The skier has a double problem in outer clothing: He must be warm enough on his way to the skiing area and riding the lift, yet not too heavily clothed while skiing, since, if he is, the exertion will make him perspire, a sure way to get chilled. So do not dress in such a way that it will be inconvenient to peel off a sweater or two.

SKI PARKA. Ski parkas are often things of beauty; much less frequently are they joys forever. Whatever style you favor, be sure of the following things: raglan-type sleeves, shoulders wide enough to accommodate sweaters underneath and still give free arm movement, full enough cut so that raising the arms doesn't jerk up the waist, zipper closure with a large enough tab on the zipper to be grasped by a gloved hand, sufficiently long sleeves to protect wrists, long enough skirt (or tight enough waistband) to prevent entry of snow under the parka in a sliding fall.

As with ski pants, the best materials for parkas are windproof, water-repellent, lightweight. Quilted parkas provide excellent warmth and are popular in the early, colder ski season and colder skiing areas, conditions in which their bulk is a secondary consideration to their warmth.

ACCESSORIES.   Ski caps, or headbands of knitted wool protect the head and ears. Fur hats, long-tailed stockingcaps and gay face masks are fun and functional, too. If it is cold enough for you to pull the ear flaps in your cap down over your ears for protection, a glimpse in a mirror may convince you that knitted headgear looks better. There are many styles, shapes, and colors of ski caps, all adequate and each with its special advantages. Only one word of caution in buying is needed: Loose fit or long visor may be the cause of your trudging up a slope to recapture a fleeing cap that has blown off in a gust of wind.

Several turtleneck T-shirts with long body and sleeves are recommended. Get them in a range of weights and materials.

If you ski in the spring, or in areas of few trees and bright winter sunlight, goggles will be needed to protect your eyes from glare. Snow blindness caused by glare from snow or ice is extremely painful, though rarely encountered in the average skier's experience; but the actinic rays of the sun, reflected from snow, can do permanent injury to unprotected eyes before one becomes aware of discomfort. Never wear breakable glass goggles. Goggles of unbreakable plastic protect the corners of the eyes as well as the pupils, and are inexpensive.

GADGETS.   There's an unending variety of gadgets for the skier, some of them useful and ingenious, others merely decorative or intriguing. The disease known as gimmick fever may attack you when you see counters loaded with good-looking gadgetry and can lead you to load yourself up with all manner of doohickeys which are harmless enough but won't do much more for you than provide you with playthings. On the other hand, there are definitely helpful gadgets, not absolutely essential but very useful—and very appealing, too. You'll find a few of them pictured on page 34.

Care of Equipment

BOOTS

Keep strong shoe trees in your boots (or clamp them in a boot press) when they are not in use. Do not dry them without trees or press to hold their shape, and do not let them dry too rapidly or in front of a fire or hot stove. Do not oil or "soap" them; this makes the leather flabby and stretches it, and the excess oil which penetrates the pores of the leather hardens when exposed to cold so that the pores stay open. One or two applications each season of a dressing recommended by the manufacturer are sufficient. Ordinary paste shoe polish, used daily, keeps boots looking well and in good condition.

GADGETS. Two excellent combination boot-press carriers, the Tyrolia (with Garmisch boots) and the EZ-3 (with Koflach boots); to the right, a plaid boot toter and below it a handled, zippered ski bag, both from Abercrombie & Fitch. Ski goggles are, from left to right, Bouton ski and sports goggles, Sea and Ski's polarized Competition goggles, Protector racing goggles with safety-glass lenses, Carrera goggles with interchangeable lenses, and Super Carrera with interchangeable lenses and built-in nose guard. To the right is a flexible cable ski lock by American Ski Corp., and bottom, left, is a fur-covered Alpine Krafts wineskin; at right, kidney-shaped leather wine *bota* from Abercrombie & Fitch. (You may load them with stronger potations, too—*Prosit!*)

POLES

Leather parts of ski poles should be kept well softened and pliable by periodic application of leather dressing or saddle soap. Two or three times a season will suffice. The wrist strap especially must be kept untwisted and pliant.

SKIS AND BINDINGS

When not in use, skis made of wood or wood laminates should be clamped together at heel and point of tip contact and a spreader block placed between them at their widest separation to preserve camber. Do not use a block or spreader which forces them apart beyond their normal separation. If the clamp used is the kind which has attachments for holding the tips of the skis, adjust the attachment to fit the upcurve as it is—don't force the tips into a sharper curve. After use, skis and bindings should be wiped dry. Never put a wet or moist ski near heat. The hinged parts of ski bindings should be lightly oiled with a thin gun oil which will not turn gummy or stiff. When not in use, skis properly clamped and blocked should be stored in a cool, dry place. Don't depend on rubber snap-on holders to keep the skis held together when not in use. These rubber gadgets are all right for carrying skis to and from the slope, but that is all they are meant for.

Nomenclature and Schematic Diagrams

Every movement and maneuver described in this book is illustrated by a photograph or a diagram or both. Everything is labeled. Much confusion results from the usual custom of sometimes calling a spade a spade, and sometimes referring to it as a club, heart, diamond, or shovel. For example, when the terms "inside ski" and "outside ski" are used exclusively to identify the skis in the execution of a turn (the inside ski being the one nearest the center of the turn, as shown in Figure 1), everything is fine until the next phase is reached and the turn becomes an S curve, when all at once the outside ski becomes the inside ski, and vice versa.

The same limitations beset those who stick to the terms "uphill ski" and "downhill ski" since a change of direction—as in a C-shaped turn—changes the names, and downhill ski becomes uphill ski.

In this book such confusions are avoided by the following means. Turns (which are the principal maneuvers in skiing) will be identified in most cases as "right turns" and "left turns." The term "right ski" will apply to the ski worn on the right foot, "left ski" to that worn on the left foot, and skis in the diagrams are marked accordingly, L and R (Figure 1).

When such a distinction is unnecessary, or tends to make the description too complicated, the terms "inside ski" and "outside ski" will be used, as well as the terms "uphill ski" and "downhill ski."

All diagrams of maneuvers show a top-down view of the skis and a cross-section of them. A black ski indicates that the entire weight of the skier is supported on that ski. Identically shaded skis indicate that the weight is equally distributed on them. A white ski is completely unweighted (though not lifted clear of the snow). Whenever it has proved feasible, the actual track of the skis through the snow has also been indicated in diagrams. And in turns where shoulder action is used, the position of the shoulders is shown, and arrows indicate their motion. In most cases, an actual top-down drawing of the skier is shown.

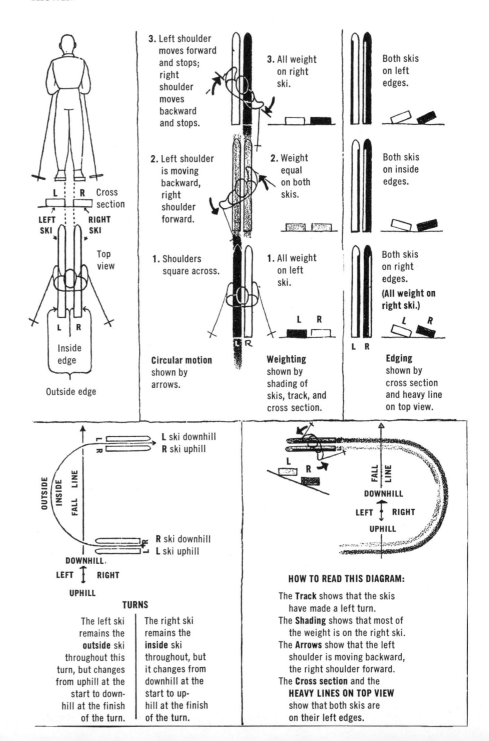

Figure 1—Nomenclature— Diagrammatic Notation

This is all you will need to know in order to study the following chapters. New words will be explained as they are introduced. Always study the diagrams, drawings, and photographs closely, observing position of skis, feet, ankles, knees, legs, body, shoulders, arms. Numbers accompanying the various elements of a diagram refer to the same numbers in the text or in the photographs.

NOTE: IN THE DIAGRAMS YOU, THE SKIER, ARE CONSIDERED TO BE AT THE TOP OF THE HILL, LOOKING DOWN. THEREFORE, AS YOU HOLD THE BOOK FOR READING, THE BOTTOM OF THE PAGE IS UPHILL, THE TOP OF THE PAGE IS DOWNHILL AND THE RIGHT OF THE SLOPE IS TO YOUR RIGHT.

Do's and Don'ts

Do keep your equipment in proper shape. If it's worth having, it's worth caring for. You'll have better skiing if you take a little more trouble in treating your gear well.

Do familiarize yourself with the simple diagrammatic notation and the nomenclature used in this book. It will aid immeasurably in the learning process.

Do take your time in buying equipment. It is better to miss one weekend of skiing than to suffer because of bad equipment for the rest of the season.

Do make sure your skis are neither too stiff nor too springy.

Do be guided in your purchases by quality and functionalism—looks are secondary.

Do work right through this book, and make sure you understand not only the how of things, but also the why.

DON'T economize in the wrong places. Poor boots and bindings can keep you from becoming a skier; lack of fancy garb and gadgets can't.

DON'T gloss over what may seem like simple exercise; everything in this book is there for a reason.

DON'T ski when you are feeling ill or when the weather is bad and snow conditions hazardous. Better to lose a weekend than earn the right to a hospital bed.

DON'T experiment with a variety of "schools" and "systems"; select one and stick to it.

DON'T overdress for skiing. It's better to shiver a little, until you warm up by skiing, than to perspire on the slope and then get chilled.

DON'T rush the learning process. You can't expect to make christies your first day, and you'll never make a good fast turn until you can make a successful slow one.

CHAPTER TWO

FIRST STEPS ON SKIS

Well, well, well. Here you are, all dressed for skiing, all equipped with nice new gear, standing on the snow at the foot of a perpendicular hill a million miles high, in constant danger of being run down by madmen skimming all about you, having trouble enough standing up in your boots, let alone on a pair of slippery boards. You think of a nice hot, stuffy movie theater, or the comfortable seat you might be occupying in front of the fireplace. "Why," you ask yourself with some asperity, "why didn't I go to St.-Tropez this winter?"

Before the end of the season you'll be standing at the top of that same hill (which has miraculously shrunk to a nice easy slope) looking down on another tyro who is experiencing the same sensations of locked or rubbery knees and hollow stomach that you can dimly recall having felt. Do you gloat? Not you; you're a skier now, and skiers are gentlemen about such things.

But it's not the end of the season yet, it's the beginning. At least it's the beginning for you—it is your first time out. Well, you think, let's get our skis on.

At this point a friend or a well-meaning stranger comes over to help you and teach you. *Shun him as the plague!* Send him away with polite thanks and, if that fails, growl at him, make faces or utter fierce and incoherent sounds. He is the bane of the nursery slope. He's not a qualified teacher, nor is he likely to be a very good skier; if he were,

Figure 2—Putting on Skis

he'd be somewhere else, with the other experts. His offer of help is probably one tenth altruism and nine tenths ego bolstering.

What you need on your first day is peace and quiet to get the feel of skis on your feet, and to experiment. So you walk to a nice, private spot, a nice, level, open space, and you put down your skis. They are usually marked L and R just in front of the binding.

Place the skis flat on the ground and parallel. Plant your poles firmly in the snow on either side of the skis. Stand between the skis and insert the toe of the left boot into the toepiece of the left ski. If the ski slides forward, you can hold it firm by hooking the snow ring of the left pole over the ski tip (Figure 2). Now complete the closing of the binding.

Follow the procedure outlined above, and put on the right ski. This will be a little harder, since one foot is already on a ski, but you will soon learn the knack.

Correct holding of the poles comes next. Place the hand with palm touching the shaft of the pole well below the hand grip and wrist strap (Figure 3a). Move the hand up through the wrist strap until the strap is well onto the wrist (Figure 3b). Then grasp the hand grip (Figure 3c). Held thus, correctly, the poles are used with the combined strength of hand and wrist, yet the strap does not cut off circulation. If the pole is accidentally dropped from the hand, it trails from the wrist strap and can be grasped again.

And now you're ready to shove off.

Figure 3—Putting on Wrist Strap

a. *Hand reaches up.*
b. *Strap is on wrist.*
c. *Grasping pole handle.*

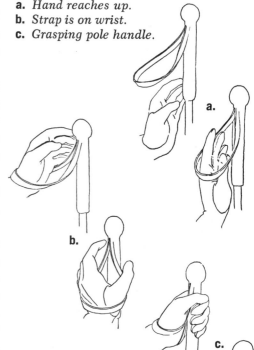

Skiing on the Level

Skiing on the level is merely a gliding walk. Suppose you want to start with your left ski. Weight is on right ski, you slide the left ski forward, glide on it as much as possible, then, before the glide stops, smoothly shift the weight forward onto the left ski and, as the glide diminishes, slide the right ski forward. The two main differences between the ski-walking step and walking without skis are these: On skis, you don't lift your foot, but slide it forward; and on skis you help your walk with the ski poles.

When you stride along the street you use your arms in what is known as "opposition"; that is, when your left foot goes forward, your right arm swings forward, and vice versa. The same is true in the walking step in skiing; as you advance your left ski, your right pole moves forward, and vice versa. The poles are planted in the snow and are given the propelling thrust with shoulder, elbow, and wrist, the shoulder doing most of the work. Keep your arms close to your body so that you get maximum leverage on the poles.

Walking on skis should be done in a relaxed and easy way. Tension, especially in the knees, will result in strain and bad balance. The price of tension is a dunking in the snow, which isn't bad but doesn't come under the head of progress.

So walk relaxed. Try to get body motion—a little "zing"—into your glide, a little rocking from ski to ski as you shift weight, a yielding of the knees as the weight comes onto first one ski, then the other, a rhythmic rolling of the shoulders as you thrust with first one pole and then the opposite pole.

Most of all, keep your body just a bit forward, *from the ankles up*. Don't lean your upper body forward while your seat sticks out behind; if you do, your knees will be stiff and you'll look like a courtier about to make a sweeping bow. This position is swell for bowing. It's also unsurpassed for tipping you over on your side if one ski goes over a slight bump (because you'll have no knee action with which to adjust to it) and it sets you up for a sit-down. Want to prove it? O.K.

Stand up. Yes, right now. Lock your knees straight, toes and heels together. Bend forward from the waist, as in a bow. Now try to bend at the knees without shifting your weight forward. See what happens? You can't do it without falling unless there's a chair behind you to catch you. But on skis you never get a chance to find this out, for the moment you make the initial movements in this sit-down stance, your skis will slide forward, leaving you behind. Get up, smile sweetly, and fill in the bathtub you've just carved in the snow. Or don't make this typical mistake in the first place.

Look at Figure 4. Note how the skier in the photographs below is walking—body slightly forward, knees flexible and easy, head up and looking forward, not down at the skis. Note the poles, close to the body so that maximum thrust is delivered.

Now look at the poor chap in Figure 5. He's using arms and legs in unison instead of in opposition. His skis are too far apart—they are not parallel; his knees are stiff; his tail is wagging out behind him; and his poles, which he has mistakenly flung out to the side for balance, are useless because he can't get any leverage on them that way. We won't show you the last picture, in which he is comfortable. Later, he will get up and try again.

Figure 4—Walking on Level

1. Right ski ahead, left pole leading.   **2.** Left ski ahead, right pole leading.

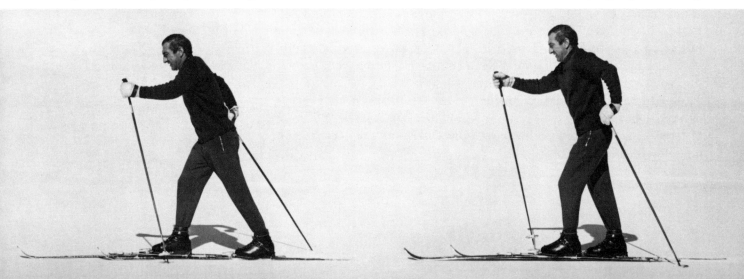

Figure 5—Wrong Walking on Level

Poles incorrectly held, right ski and right arm are moved forward together (not in opposition), skis neither close nor parallel, knees stiff.

Let's face the fact that you are going to fall. It's no sin, and it won't hurt you.

If you feel yourself falling, make a normal effort to retain equilibrium, but don't fight the fall to the bitter end. You'll wind up in a tangle of skis, poles and cuss words if you do. Instead, let yourself fall relaxed, keeping your poles out of your way, and falling to the side, when possible. And when you're down, stay down for a moment—don't struggle.

So you're down—you've fallen. Let's suppose you're on level terrain. How to get up? First roll over on your back with feet in the air. Then get your skis parallel and pointing in the same direction. Get them close together. Roll onto your side, and draw your skis up as close to your body as possible, knees bent to the maximum. You are going to push yourself upright with the help of your poles, so when drawing up your legs against your body, do it in such a way that your feet are drawn up under your seat, not in front of it or behind it. If your feet are forward of your seat, your skis will slide out from under you as you get your weight on them; if your feet are too far back, the skis will slip out behind you.

Once your skis are properly drawn up, take the wrist straps of the poles off your wrists, and grasp both poles together, just below the hand grips, in your free hand (that is, the hand on the side you are not lying on). Grasp both poles in the other hand just above the snow ring. Now plant both poles together in the snow, gripped as described, about on a line with your head, and fairly close to it. Planted firmly and held in this way, you can use them to push yourself up. You may want to change the placing of the hands and the planting of the poles, depending on the length of your arms and the length of your poles. Remember, though, the object is to be able to use the poles to push yourself up. Do *not* try to *pull* yourself up. You have more strength and will have better balance in pushing than in pulling up.

If you do fall downhill on a slope (see Figures 6 and 7), roll onto your back, turn around so that your head is uphill of your

Falling
and Getting Up

1. Down.　　　　**2.** Rolling over.　　　　**3.** Drawing parallel skis up to body.

Figure 6—Falling and Getting Up on a Slope

4. Planting poles.　　　　**5.** Pushing up.　　　　**6.** Up.

body, swing your skis downhill, get them at right angles to the slope, then pull them up close to the body and proceed as above. If they aren't at right angles to the slope, the skis will run away while you're trying to get up, thus producing an effect more suitable to adagio dancing than to skiing. One faceful of snow can cure you of failing to place your skis across the slope, but why learn the hard way?

Step Turn

Let us assume you have managed to walk along with some success, and you come to the end of your clear, level space. You want to turn. You will discover very soon that the degree of turning you can do with one ski is limited by the fact that the skis will cross if you turn one at all far. Crossed skis make the shape of a letter X, which marks the spot where you either fall or uncross them and find yourself still headed in the same direction and no turn accomplished.

Figure 7—Wrong Way Up

All the skier's straining will come to naught; as soon as he's up a little higher, his skis will shoot forward and he'll be down again.

Figure 8—Step Turn

Four phases.

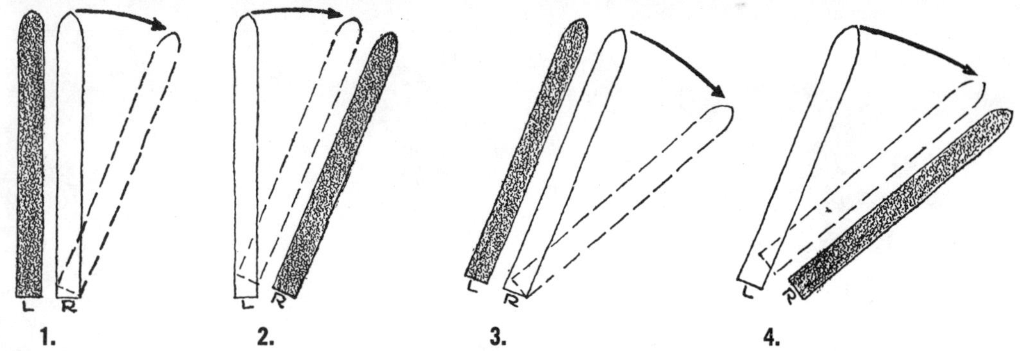

1. 2. 3. 4.

Here is how to do it. For a right turn, lift the right ski off the snow, very slightly, mostly at the tip (the ski pivots from the tail end) and turn your foot outward a little. Plant that ski on the ground, put your weight on it, and lift and pivot the left ski so that it comes parallel and close to the right. Repeat until you have turned the desired amount (Figure 8).

Now try to combine the forward walking step with the step turn. With a little practice, you'll be able to execute a reasonably smooth circle, sliding forward on the turned ski, sliding a little forward again as you bring the other ski parallel to it.

And now for an axiom of what we deem to be priceless advice. *Don't ever, until you're an expert skier, make two turns in succession which are in the same direction.* If you start with a right turn, make a left turn before you make another right. And vice versa. There are thousands of temporarily stopped skiers today whose block is that they can execute a maneuver in only one direction, or better in one direction than in the other. It is a hard block to break; it is easy to avoid suffering from it if you practice every step and turn in both directions, initiating the movements with first one ski and then the other. If you do develop unevenly, so that a right turn, for example, is easier for you than a left turn, then withstand the temptation to demonstrate your skill, and practice the left turn until you can do it as easily as the right turn; this should be the only exception to the axiom. Once you've equalized matters, alternate right and left again.

Kick Turn

The kick turn is the best and quickest way to reverse direction and is part of the repertory of every good skier. It looks tricky but is easily learned if you learn it right. Once you know it, you'll wonder how you ever found it difficult.

To kick-turn to the left, first plant your poles firmly in the snow as shown in Figure 9-1. Now kick your left foot forward and up—swing it high, as though you were trying to kick a field goal. You must kick it high enough so that the heel of the ski just clears the surface of the snow when the ski points straight up (Figure 9-2) and far enough in front of you so that the heel of the left ski lines up with the tip of the right ski. The height of the ski from heel to binding, plus the weight of the ski and boot, may make this seem like a tough job. It isn't, though,

1. Planting poles.   **2.** Kick.   **3.** Left ski turning toward new direction.

Figure 9—Kick Turn

4. Halfway around—tip to heel.   **5.** Bringing second ski and pole around.   **6.** Finished turn.

if you use this simple trick: Swing the kicking foot back a bit first, just as you swing a golf club or tennis racket back before your stroke, and then *swing* your foot; don't try to lift it by main force.

When the left ski is up, don't stop at the top of the swing, but turn the ski as though you were pivoting it on its heel (Figure 9-3), and let it come down to the snow in its new direction, so that the skis will be close together and parallel, tip to heel (Figure 9-4). Now lift the entire length of the right ski clear of the snow a few inches and swing it around (Figure 9-5) until it can be placed on the snow alongside the left ski and parallel to it. The right pole comes around with the right ski. You are facing in the new direction (Figure 9-6). Practice kick turns to right and left. Get plenty of swing into the kick. Learn to make the turn in one fluid series of motions, not as separate, jerky ones.

Traversing Uphill

"So far so good," you say, "but what about actual skiing, downhill?" Well, we'll assume you've walked and step-turned, done a few stability exercises and kick-turned enough to be somewhat acquainted with your skis, and that you are looking tentatively yet with increasing frequency at a nice gentle slope and thinking you'd like to try it. But you have to get up first. The simplest way up is called traversing (Figures 10 and 11). This merely means that instead of attacking the hill head on (in which case your skis would slide backwards), you angle up the hill by going at a diagonal to the slope. If, in doing so, your skis tend to slip sideways down the slope, tilt your skis slightly so that the uphill edges bite into the snow. If you are going up a hill in a traverse from the lower left of the hill to the upper right of it, for instance, the hill is to your left, and you would edge both skis on their left-hand (uphill) edges. You can do this properly only if your knees are nicely flexed, your weight centered on your skis (leaning neither

Figure 10—Uphill Traverse

2. Uphill ski is forward and planted; downhill ski will now move ahead.

1. Downhill ski is forward; uphill ski starts to come forward.

Figure 11—Uphill Traverse

3. Right ski ahead, left ski ready to advance.

2. Midstride.

1. Left ski has been planted; right ski starts forward.

Figure 12—Wrong Uphill Traverse

Note flat skis, not edged to maintain secure climbing; body leaning forward from hips; skier trying to push uphill with poles.

forward nor back), and your knees pressed in very slightly toward the slope. Your body should be at right angles to the skis, and leaning neither toward the slope nor away from it.

Let's suppose you've traversed a third of your way up the hill in this way, and you come to an obstruction. Bring the skis squarely across the slope, then do a kick turn *always turning downhill, with the downhill ski doing the kick, which is much easier than attempting an uphill kick turn,* and traverse again in the opposite direction.

Half Side Step

If you have difficulty traversing your hill without backsliding, you can make a less oblique traverse. Or if you want to get up more rapidly, you can use the half side step (Figure 13). Imagine yourself at the

Figure 13—Half Side Step

1. Right ski planted; left ski has moved up and forward.
2. Left ski planted; right ski moving up and forward.

foot of a flight of stairs. You stand sideways, with your feet parallel to the edges of the stairs. The half side step is a combination of this sideways stair climbing and the regular skiing walk. Get thrust with your downhill pole, keep the skis edged into the slope so that they don't slide sideways, and remember to step forward as well as up with each step. The uphill ski reaches forward and up while the downhill ski holds your weight. Then the uphill ski takes the weight (edged uphill and firmly planted) while the downhill ski is brought up alongside it and ahead of it, as in walking on the level. Arms and body are used in a rhythmical way, as they were in walking, and shoulders are kept squarely forward and at equal height.

3. Track shows uphill traverse leading into half side step.

Figure 14—Full Side Step

1. Left ski planted; right ski and pole moving uphill.
2. Right ski planted; left ski and pole moving uphill.

Side Step

The quickest way up (and the most tiring—but it's the only way on very steep slopes) is the side step. This is our friend the sideways stair climb, done without any forward progress whatever, just right up the slope (Figure 14).

There is one other way to climb a slope. This is the herringbone step, but we'll come to that later. Right now, you want to ski down this hill we've just climbed.

Schuss

The act of skiing straight down a hill, without turning or checking speed, is called downhill running, or, at high speeds, the schuss. (Let us flatter ourselves, and simplify matters for the nonce by calling all straight downhill running schussing.) Your first schuss will feel like flying. So will your second—and your thousandth. That's one of the wonderful things about skiing.

The ideal setup for your first schuss is a short hill, with a gentle, even slope, a level starting place at its top, and a long, level runout at the bottom. If you can find it, well and good. Climb to the top, using traverses linked by kick turns, the half side step or the side step. Once on the level at the top, do another kick turn, walk to the start of the slope, and you're ready.

Most likely, though, you won't find a ready-made small hill. Select a hill whose lower slope is gentle, and where there is a good runout. Go up it fifty feet or so (that's enough for your first schuss) and get your

1. Planting poles downhill.   **2.** Stepping around.   **3.** Ready to go.

Figure 15—Turning on Slope to Schuss

skis at right angles, across the slope. Make sure you have a firm stance, so that you can take your poles out of the snow without sliding in either direction. Plant your poles downhill, lean on them, and stepturn around until your skis are pointing straight down. Your poles will keep you from sliding forward (Figure 15).

Whether you start from the top of a small hill, or from part way up a slope, once you are turned around and your skis are pointing straight downhill the procedure is the same.

Here is the correct schuss position: skis one to two inches apart, one ski a few inches in advance of the other, weight equal on both skis, knees directly above skis—that is, neither knocked inward nor bowed out. Skis flat, not edged. Poles are held firmly (but not with a tiring death grip), arms comfortably out to the sides to facilitate balance; pole tips down near the snow but not dragging; the poles make a V out behind you; your elbows are a little out from the body, just enough so that the poles make their V without your having to bend your wrists. Hands are at about waist height; elbows, though bent, are relaxed, not tense or locked.

Flex your knees up and down a few times; as you flex them, keep your backside in and flat, not thrust out behind you, and your weight evenly distributed fore and aft, and with the heels flat down on the skis. Try to bend forward from the ankles a bit so that you can keep your body perpendicular to the slope. The steeper the slope, the greater the speed; the greater the speed, the more you'll lean into it for poised balance, but don't crouch as if you were going to sit. Bend forward from the ankles, with the knees limber, and not from the waist.

Now—are you set? Let 'er rip. Don't look at the tips of your skis, but ahead of you. Head up. If your knees are stiff, the least unevenness of ground can tip you over. If you weight one ski more than the other, or advance the lead ski too far, your balance will be bad. If you give way to timidity and lean back, your skis will go out from under you. Take it

1. Side.　　　　　　**2.** Back.　　　　　　**3.** Front.

Figure 16—Correct Schuss Position

nice and easy, ride the boards with flexible knees and courage, and you'll sail down the slope with ease.

Study Figure 16. It shows the correct schuss position. Toes, knees, and chin are in a straight line. The line is at right angles to the slope. This used to be known as vorlage, a much misunderstood word, as you can easily tell if you observe misinformed skiers who ski down gentle slopes leaning way out over their ski tips or crouching as though they were going to ski through a barrel. Logic tells us that when the body is leaning too far forward, the slightest slowing of the skis, caused by changing terrain or a patch of slow snow, will promptly pitch the skier forward on his face. Similarly, if he is leaning back, he is in constant danger of having his skis shoot out from under him, leaving him behind. The ideal stance is one in which the axis of the body is at right angles to the slope, with the skier's weight squarely centered on the skis. In this position he is ideally poised to compensate for variations in speed or gradient by shifting his weight forward or back. High-speed skiers sometimes have to lean forward beyond the vertical line in order to overcome wind resistance, but the net result of the forces involved is still the placing of the skier's center of gravity over the center of the skis.

Now look at the people in Figure 17. Poor Mr. A thinks he has fine erect stance just because his head is forward. But he has too much ballast out behind. Friend B is plain scared and is sitting back. This weight to the rear of the skis is an abomination in the eyes of the god of skiing. And C is suffering from the delusion that to get your weight forward you have to stand on your toes. D is in racing stance on a gentle slope, which makes as much sense as wearing spurs to ride a hobby horse.

Now look at Figure 16 again. Study the position of heels, hands,

A.

B.

Figure 17—Wrong Schuss

A. Stiff—bending forward from waist; hands and head forward.
B. Leaning back—ideal for sitting, bad for skiing.
C. On toes (hanging from cables).
D. Racing stance on a gentle slope; pointless and unstable.

C.

head, back, hips, knees, ankles. If you can, put your skis on indoors, in front of a mirror, and assume the pose—but relaxed. Tenseness and skiing don't go together.

D.

Let's suppose you've mastered your first hill. You can schuss it with comfort and ease and are ready for new hills to conquer. You're ready to learn the herringbone then, since, to develop wind and stability, you should climb before you schuss instead of depending on tows or lifts.

The herringbone is used to go straight up a hill and is useful on all hills that are not so steep as to require the side step. It's quicker and more direct than the traverses with kick turns, and it will keep you out of the way of skiers on their way down a slope since you won't have to crisscross it.

This manner of climbing gets its name from the pattern it makes on

Herringbone

Figure 18—Herringbone

Right ski going forward. (Note track.)

the snow (Figure 18). The skis are in V position, heels close together, tips spread wide. Weight is on the inside edges of both skis. Poles are thrust into the snow behind the skis and are used "in opposition," as in walking; that is, the left pole supports and thrusts while the right ski is advanced, and vice versa. Plant each ski down firmly with each step, lift the heel of one ski over the other, and forge up the hill Charlie Chaplin fashion. The knees are bent well forward and are not sprung outward at all. If you maintain the proper knee position, strong edging will be easy.

A Time for Fun

Having come this far, you'll inevitably feel that there has been a certain amount of drudgery involved. Now is a good time to shake off that feeling of earnest hard work and, at the same time, to get to know your skis a bit better. You can have fun while you do this, and end up with the feeling that you and the skis have become a unit, rather than separate entities in an uneasy truce in treacherous surroundings that are waiting to trap you into falling.

An excellent way to limber up when you first get out on a slope, to get the relaxed and comfortable feeling you want on your skis, and also to cover territory, is to combine pushing and gliding while walking. This is really a sort of beginner's cross-country stride. Look at Figure 19. You will see that the skier uses his entire body, legs, and pole push, too, in order to get up enough speed to glide. Before the

Figure 19—Pushing and Gliding While Walking (A Cross-Country Step)

3. Glide.   **2.** Push.   **1.** Stride.

Figure 20—Single-Ski Balancing Exercise on Gentle, Smooth Slope. Alternate from One Ski to the Other, Rhythmically

glide comes to a stop, he resumes his striding and pole pushing. Do this and strive for a rhythm in it. You may wish to count in your head: "One, two, three—glide; one, two, three—glide . . ." etc. You can get up quite a bit of speed this way and you will find that you automatically achieve a sort of rolling motion, not unlike that of a sea captain striding the deck of his ship.

When you've warmed up with your gliding walk, find a gentle and smooth slope of even gradient, and try single-ski balancing as shown in Figure 20. Again, you are doing this for the purpose of getting to feel comfortable and happy on your skis, and you'll find that it adds a bit of fun to what would otherwise be, by now, a too-simple schuss. When you've gotten so that you can alternate from one ski to the other without losing your balance, try to get rhythm into it and dance down the slope.

A final limbering exercise and one that has considerable utility, too, is skating (Figure 21). It's not unlike ice skating at a rink. On skis, however, you've got the help of your poles and considerably more natural stability than you enjoy on the blades of skates. You'll know you've mastered skating and have become better buddies with your skis when you can have fun on a slope by starting to schuss and then, before you get to the level, just as you are slowing down, skating the rest of the·way to maintain speed.

Finally, before taking off your skis for a rest or a coffee break, stand on the level, firmly plant your poles as shown in Figure 22, and then—

Figure 21—Skating

Right to left: the four phases of skating on skis. Note opened tips forming skis into slight "V" and vigorous, rhythmic body and pole action.

just for the hell of it—kick up your heels behind you, alternately, making the kicks more swinging and vigorous as you gain a feeling of security. It's a great way to loosen up the socks, warm the toes, get the blood circulating, and attain poise in motion. If you have any doubts about the last statement, try a good, strong mule kick without the poles for support; the snow will be very cooling to your face.

We beg you—as you limber up and learn to relax while gliding, balancing alternately on one ski and then the other, skating, kicking—to please, above all, have fun! One reason many children learn skiing as rapidly as they do is that the wee tads will simply not be serious. In having fun on skis, in playing in the outdoor playground which is a snowscape, they quickly get the hang of the skis and how they and the skis can be a happy combination. That's what you too should do.

Figure 22—Backward Heel Kick

With firmly planted poles and on level snow, vigorously kick up your skis behind you, first one ski, then the other.

Do's and Don'ts

Do keep skis parallel in walking, or you'll do an involuntary split or X.

Do use your poles with the wrist strap. Serious injury can result from a pole which slides through your hand and jabs you in the stomach or eye. In a fall, the pole used without wrist strap becomes a dangerous weapon.

Do refuse firmly all offers of "instruction" from well-meaning people. Only a qualified teacher knows how to teach.

Do practice all maneuvers in both directions.

Do be sure you are firmly "planted" before attempting a kick turn.

Do keep your shoulders square in traversing uphill and in doing the side steps. Dropping the downhill shoulder is a common bad habit, hard to unlearn and easy to avoid beforehand.

Do keep the skis tip to heel at the halfway point of the kick turn like this:

Do the suggested stability and familiarity exercises for relaxing good fun and to forget that you are on skis.

DON'T walk on "eggs"; walking on skis, like all skiing, is free flowing, makes use of the entire body, is more a big-stepped stride than a tentative and mincing walk.

DON'T edge out in the schuss. This is a common fault, caused by bowing out the knees.

DON'T be a "one-way-turn" skier.

DON'T *ever* put your poles into the snow in front of you in order to stop.

DON'T be a backslider. Be patient and make reasonable uphill traverses. If you want to go up steeply, use the herringbone or side step.

DON'T look at your ski tips; look ahead, to see what's coming.

DON'T try to make a kick turn with a bent leg, like this:

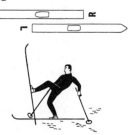

CHAPTER THREE

LEARNING TO STOP AND TURN

Snowplow

So far, your schussing has been done on hills where there is a sufficiently long and level runout so that you naturally come to a stop. Your speed in the schuss has been a matter of the steepness of the hill and the quality of the snow. Literally, you haven't been skiing; you've been taking a ride on skis.

The snowplow is a means of slowing down or stopping at low speeds. As such, it is extremely useful. But it is much more than just that. The snowplow is the base on which all good skiing rests. It is to skiing what the egg is to the chicken—the beginning of everything. Many is the amateur and near-beginner who considers the snowplow irksome drudgery, to be quickly learned and then never again used except in an emergency. You have to know the snowplow to do the snowplow turn, and you have to know the snowplow turn before you can think of graduating from the beginners' ranks.

Remember the herringbone, for going up the hill? The snowplow is, in a sense, its exact reverse. In the snowplow the skis are in V position with the toes together and the heels apart. The word "snowplow" is descriptive of the action of the skis in this V position: they offer resistance to the snow and slow your forward motion or stop it.

Before explaining how the snowplow is done, let us consider the prosaic subject of a solid pound of butter and a knife. Slicing a cut across the surface of the butter with the knife blade is easy (Figure 23a). That's like your ski going downhill straight. Moving the flat of the knife over the butter creates a little more friction and takes more force in wielding the knife. If the force isn't increased, the knife will move more slowly in this position. That's like the broadside of your ski presented to the slope, as in the snowplow position. But if the knife blade is absolutely flat to the butter, a slight bump on the surface of the butter will tilt the knife down into the butter (Figure 23d). Thus, if the skis are absolutely flat in the snowplow, the outside edges may catch and the skier will complete the descent on his face. Now, if the knife blade is edged so that the leading edge is raised a very, very little, it can be stroked over the surface of the butter without catching on its front edge at all (Figure 23b); but if it is edged too much, it will start to pile up butter and will move sideways, along the line of the blade, more easily than it will forward (Figure 23c). Similarly, in a snow-

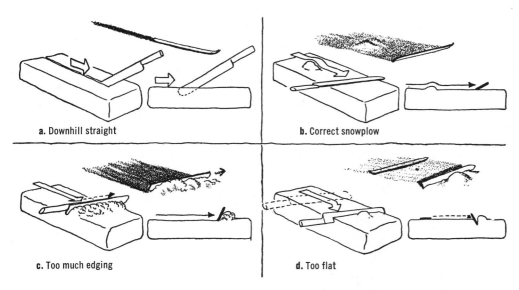

a. Downhill straight

b. Correct snowplow

c. Too much edging

d. Too flat

Figure 23—The "Knife and Butter" Analogy

plow, if the skis are edged just right they will stroke the surface of the snow and not pile up snow under themselves; if they are edged too much, they will pile up snow for a little and then cross, and the skier once more will be doing a nose plow down the slope.

If the knife-and-butter analogy doesn't ring the bell with you, try, next time you're in the tub, stroking the surface of the water with the flat of your hand, tilting your hand at various angles to the water and observing the effect. Or, riding in a car, hold your flattened palm out the window and tilt it at various angles against the wind; you will get the feel of the snowplow's effect.

Back to you on the snow. Here are the things to remember when doing the snowplow: Tips of skis close together, tails of skis spread out in a V, your heels flat down on the skis, knees well bent and body right smack over the center of the skis, but with some pressure on the heels. Look ahead, not down at your skis, and *keep those knees bent.* Unless you do, you won't be able to keep an effective V position. You can curve the back a very little. Keep weight and body contour symmetrically arranged and equal on both skis.

Understand it? Ready to try it? Good. Go up your practice hill and start your schuss down. As you begin to slow up on the level runout, force out both heels into the snowplow V, edging the skis very slightly on their inner edges, and hold the position until you come to a stop. If your skis cross, edge less. If the snowplow doesn't slow you down, separate the heels more to make a wider V and increase the weight on the heels. If the runout is packed hard or is icy, you may edge a little more. Figure 24 shows a correct snowplow.

Once you've learned to use the snowplow to stop your runout on the

Figure 24—Snowplow

1. Front.

2. Side.

3. Back.

level, you are ready to start controlling your speed while descending a hill. Go to the top of your hill, start down in good schuss position, and then gradually force out the tails of your skis into the snowplow V. Start your snowplow before you attain full speed in the schuss. Come down the hill in the snowplow, slowly.

Try it again. This time let yourself get up more speed before you snowplow. Start your snowplow gently, so that you slow gradually. Before you get to the bottom of the hill, stop pushing out on your heels and the skis will run back together again, so that you can finish the hill with a schuss. Then snowplow to a stop on the level.

In doing the snowplow, watch these salient points, which are the most common causes of errors and trouble: 1. Skis must be equally weighted and equally edged. 2. Hands are held waist high. 3. Poles should maintain a V position during the plow. 4. Knees should not be locked together in knock-kneed position, or bowed out. 5. Keep ski tips close together, or plow will not slow or stop you. 6. Edge enough to feel the braking action of skis on snow, but not so much that your skis will ride on their edges and cross. 7. Keep eyes off skis—look ahead of you, at what's coming. 8. And keep your rump tucked in flat.

This is how to know when you're well on the way to mastery of the snowplow: You should be able to come down a fairly good grade in snowplow position so slowly that you can, by widening the snowplow a little, edging a trifle more, and pressing down on the heels, stop at any point.

If you really want to make your snowplow neat and handy, you can employ a refinement called lift. It will help your snowplow by making it much easier to assume the proper V position, and it will be especially helpful in deep snow. More important still, lift is a major element in advanced technique, and learning it now, at slow, snowplow speed, will repay you many times over in the maneuvers to come.

1   2

Figure 25—Wrong Snowplow

1. Only right ski plowing; tips of skis are apart.
2. Locked knees; stiff arms pressed to body; overedging; tips touching.

Figure 26—Snowplow Track

Note schuss and snowplow alternating.

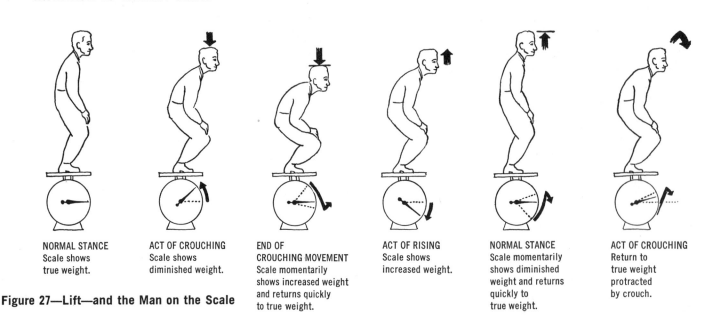

NORMAL STANCE
Scale shows
true weight.

ACT OF CROUCHING
Scale shows
diminished weight.

END OF
CROUCHING MOVEMENT
Scale momentarily
shows increased weight
and returns quickly
to true weight.

ACT OF RISING
Scale shows
increased weight.

NORMAL STANCE
Scale momentarily
shows diminished
weight and returns
quickly to
true weight.

ACT OF CROUCHING
Return to
true weight
protracted
by crouch.

Figure 27—Lift—and the Man on the Scale

What Is Lift?

In essence, lift is the momentary unweighting of both skis. It is a rising (or, rather, raising) of the body, followed immediately by a sinking back to the flexed-knee, downhill running position. In the "rise" part of the lift, the body does not come erect all the way, and there is no spring from the feet, as in jumping. The object is to raise and lower the body smoothly in such a way that the skis will momentarily be carrying a lighter load. The load will be lightest at the instant when the "rise" of the lift has reached its greatest elevation, and just as the sinking back to normal position commences. The correct lift is executed by first sinking a little lower (very little lower) than normal running position, then lifting, then sinking back to normal position. It is a measured, smooth, and continuous down-up-down.

To understand the physical principles involved in the unweighting of the skis through lift, consider the man on the scale in Figure 27. In the first picture, he is in normal running position. The scale registers his true weight. In the second picture, he is in the act of crouching lower. During the crouching movement the scale registers less than his true weight. In the third picture, he has come to rest in the crouch position (that is, the "down" part of the down-up-down which constitutes the lift). As he comes to rest, the scale will momentarily show more than his true weight (because of inertia) and will then show his true weight again. In the fourth picture, he is in the act of rising. During the rising movement the scale shows more than his true weight. In the fifth picture, he has stopped his rising motion. Momentarily the scale shows less than his true weight, then it quickly returns to the true-weight reading. In the last picture, he is starting to crouch again. Now, note this carefully: If, at the moment when the rise stops (fifth picture) and the scale shows less than true weight, the man immediately starts to crouch again, *he can protract the length of time during which the scale shows less than his true weight.*

It is this period of diminished pressure on the skis (on the scale, in the illustrative example) that one achieves by employing the lift. It is at this time that the skis can most easily be turned.

A perfect example of the effect of lift is regularly experienced when one rides in a fast elevator. As it starts up, one's apparent weight increases; when it attains uniform speed, weight is normal; when it comes to a stop, apparent weight decreases. Conversely, going down, weight is decreased during the acceleration of descent; it is normal at uniform speed; it increases when the elevator stops.

We're now ready to learn—in slow motion and on the level—just how effective lift can be in going from a schuss position to the correct snowplow position. Standing on the level, skis parallel, plant the poles to the sides and a bit forward, as shown in Figure 28, picture 1. The body is in the somewhat crouched position that is illustrated, comparable to the third picture of the man on the scale in Figure 27. Now lift (as in Figure 28, picture 2) and during the period of comparative weightlessness, fan out the heels of the skis into the snowplow position. When you first try this, most of your weightlessness will be achieved by some dependence on the poles. What you are striving for, however, is to have the poles merely handy for stability, with the lift alone achieving the condition of near weightlessness that makes the fanning out of the ski heels easy.

This is a good way to learn the feel of lift and how to employ it in making a snowplow easy, but you'll be gratified to know that it is far easier to accomplish in motion, during an actual descent of a slope.

Figure 28—Practicing Snowplow Lift on the Level

1. Poles planted for stability, skier crouched.
2. *Lift* . . .
3. . . . and fan out heels of skis into snowplow position while weightlessness is prolonged by the skier's sinking down from the full extension of his lift.

1. 2. 3.

1. Schuss position, with knees limber and body a bit lower than slope requires.

Figure 29—Lifting into a Snowplow

2. Maximum lift to achieve weightlessness.

3. Skier has easily stroked the heels of the skis into snowplow position as he prolongs weightlessness by sinking back into correct snowplow posture.

Lift in the Snowplow

To get back to the snowplow. Try the following when you want to go from schuss to snowplow: As you are on your way down the hill, decide on the exact spot where you want to start your snowplow. As you approach the spot, sink down a little lower, then *lift*—and then, at the exact moment when your lift has reduced your weight to a minimum, form your V while prolonging low weight by sinking back down to normal stance. The skis will be virtually unweighted as you heel out into the snowplow position, and they will freely and easily stroke the snow, instead of forcing their way through it.

And now you are skiing. You are in control. That is one of the major thrills of the sport, and as you ski more and witness the antics of other skiers who risk their skins and yours by swooping down a slope out of control, wherever their skis carry them, you will understand why the real skier is he who can make his skis obey his will.

The next steps in the skiing progression are the downhill turns, but before we go on to them let us consider some of the dynamics of skis on snow, and of the human body while skiing. Understanding these underlying principles will make learning faster and easier.

Interim Thoughts on Dynamics of Skis and Skiing

The entire realm of skiing divides itself into two parts, straight skiing and turns. Straight skiing—that is, walking and schuss—is used to cover ground. Turns are used to change direction, to maintain control, and to alter speed.

As has been said, the correct schuss position is with the skier's center of gravity centered on the skis; that is, with his body at right angles to the slope. Another way of saying this is that a straight line drawn through the axis of the schussing skier's body should be at right angles to the slope on which he skis. We have stressed flexibility of the

Figure 30—Bumps and Dips

knees, which are the key to skiing correctly, and their importance is apparent in considering this matter of keeping the weight correctly centered. Suppose you are going down an uneven slope, with rises and dips. If your knee action is correct, your shoulders should draw a straight line parallel to the slope while your knees flex in response to the unevenness in the surface (Figure 30). If you are too far forward with your weight, the body's hinges (ankles, knees, hips) have to be set rigidly to maintain the position, and should your skis strike a patch of loose snow which slows them abruptly, you would pitch forward and fall. On the other hand, if your weight is too far back, you are in constant danger of being left behind by your skis. Correct stance means the maintaining of a free, loose-jointed posture, vertical to the skis, so that you can respond to every variation in terrain.

Finer points will come to you automatically with practice, things such as the deeper crouching you do temporarily when lateral balance is threatened, but the prime principle of straight skiing is the easy, relaxed stance, with plenty of spring in the knees.

We have talked of the right angle made by the skier's body and the slope. There is another important right angle involved in skiing, and one which is too little appreciated. That is the right angle the leg forms with the cross-section of the ski: a straight line joining knee, shin, and ankle should be at right angles to a line drawn through the ski from edge to edge.*

Study Figure 31. On the level, the ski is flat and the leg upright, forming a right angle. Standing or skiing on the side of a hill, the skis are edged uphill and the body is upright, neither bending in toward the

---

* This rule does not hold for the stem position or in angulation, as will be explained.

Figure 31—Stability Right Angle

1. On level. **2.** On a slope. **3.** Speed turn.

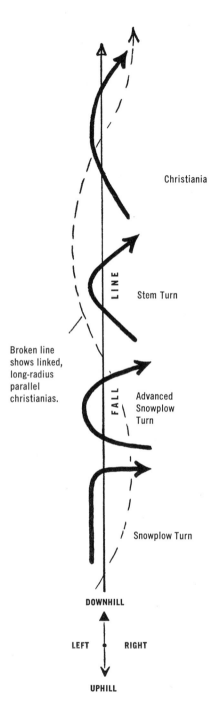

Christiania

LINE

Stem Turn

Broken line
shows linked,
long-radius
parallel
christianias.

FALL

Advanced
Snowplow
Turn

Snowplow Turn

DOWNHILL

LEFT ● RIGHT

UPHILL

Figure 32—Turns

slope nor leaning out and away from it. Again, in this traverse position, legs and skis form a right angle. In the high-speed turns, the skis bank the turn (like the wings of a plane) and the body leans in toward the center of the turn to overcome centrifugal pull.* As a result, the legs and the skis form a right angle.

This matter is extremely important, since the bending of the ankle from side to side, either in or out, weakens the linkage of hinges and levers formed by the skier's body, legs, and feet.

The theory on which this entire book is based is that it is always better, i.e., easier and more stable, to ski on two skis than on one; that the best position for the skier, at any given time, is that position in which he can rapidly and easily adjust himself to both expected and unexpected changes of speed, slope, and terrain; and that these desirable conditions are best met when the skier is poised squarely on the center of both skis, the body relaxed, the shoulders at equal height, the mechanism of spine, hips, knees, and ankles always in its most firm and most flexible position (i.e., symmetrical and centered). We mention this here for two reasons: first, we feel the student will learn faster and better if he understands the why of things; second, because some schools of skiing urge, under various circumstances, the dropping of one shoulder, the twisting or bending to the side of hips, and even the lifting of a ski from the snow while in motion. It is our belief that such expedients, which may produce results on packed slopes, or when all else fails, are contrary to the best interests and fastest development of a thorough skiing technique, capable of use under all conditions, safe, secure, and scientifically sound.

Now let us consider the matter of skiing turns.

There are three families of turns in skiing: static turns, slow-speed turns, and high-speed turns. The static turns are used solely for changing direction. The slow-speed turns are used for changing direction and decreasing speed. The high-speed turns are used for changing direction and maintaining control. (You already know the static turns, those done while not in forward motion. They are the step turn and the kick turn.)

It is when forward motion, centrifugal pull, and the force of gravity pulling downhill act on the skis and skier that new elements enter the picture. They are not many, and they are easy to understand. A ski

---

* Here, and elsewhere in this book, we use the expression "lean in" to describe the position of the body during speed turns. The body does lean in, as shown and described in pictures and text, but the weight is always predominantly on the outside ski of the turn. Most teachers agree that the learner's natural tendency is to hug the slope during a turn, in the mistaken notion that in that way lies safety. It is instinctive to bend the body in toward the slope and away from the seeming danger on the downhill side. As a result, the pupil bends the body and unwittingly transfers his weight to the ski on the inside of the turn. To overcome this tendency, many teachers admonish their pupils to lean out. By this they mean "keep the weight on the outside ski of the turn, and the body upright with respect to the skis." It should be clear, however, that when the skis are edged, as in a speed turn, the skier's body, which is upright with respect to the skis, will be at an angle with respect to the snow.

dropped on a hillside and allowed to slide away will take the shortest way down a hill. This line is called the fall line. When you schuss straight down, you are following the fall line for that particular part of the hill. When you ski at an angle to the fall line, whether uphill or down, you're traversing. In a slow-speed turn, you turn away from the fall line if you have been skiing in it, or toward it if you have been skiing a traverse. The slow-speed turn is initiated by unweighting one ski somewhat, placing it in the direction you want to go, then putting most of your weight on it. Some lift and a circular motion of the upper body are used to make the skis turn. Slow-speed turns are of fairly short radius.

High-speed turns are usually of wider radius and remain fairly close to the fall line, crossing it from side to side. They can, however, be of very short radius, sharp and abrupt. Such turns are accomplished mainly with body motion and exact knee action. Lift is used to unweight both skis simultaneously, so that the turn can be started with both skis parallel (except in what we call the basic christiania, in which the turn is initiated with the slight stemming of one ski). All these turns can be done most easily at considerable speed.

You have undoubtedly seen spectacular action photographs and movies of the high-speed turns and may be dismayed at the prospect of trying to learn to do them. Be reassured and be happy. The very first slow-speed turn you are going to learn, and the most basic and fundamental turn in the building of a sound skiing technique, is also the one which, properly executed, duplicates at slow speed the body and shoulder motions of the long-radius parallel turn, the fastest, prettiest turn of them all. It is called the snowplow turn, and the more thoroughly you learn it, the more rapid your later progress will be. It has the beauty of being learnable bit by bit; that is, you can learn the elements involved one at a time, while performing it.

Snowplow Turn

Remember how you did the snowplow? The weight was equal on both skis, the body symmetrical. Now do a slow snowplow on your practice hill, and shift the weight onto one ski. You will promptly turn. This is not a snowplow turn yet; it is turning while doing the snowplow, which is quite different, but it *is* a turn, your first while in downhill motion.

Suppose you want to try a turn away from the fall line to the right. Start straight down the practice hill with your skis in the snowplow position. Now shift all your weight onto your left ski, at the same time edging it a little more on its inside edge. You will make a right turn. The reason is simple: in the snowplow position, the left ski is pointed across the slope toward the right. If you put all your weight on it, it will carry you in that direction.

Similarly, for a left turn, put all your weight on your right ski.

In these turns, the weighted, outside ski should move a bit ahead of the inside ski, while the points are kept close to each other throughout the turn—that is, preserving the V.

For some people, the weight shift and the turning are stubborn matters to learn. If you experience difficulty, there is a strong likelihood that one or more of the following pointers will help you out.

Both knees must be bent, that is flexed, yet they must be limber, not locked in position. The outside knee should be bent the most, but the inside knee must be sufficiently bent to keep the inside ski from edging sharply, which would cause it to cross the outside ski. A common failure is inability to transfer the weight to the outside ski. Most fre-

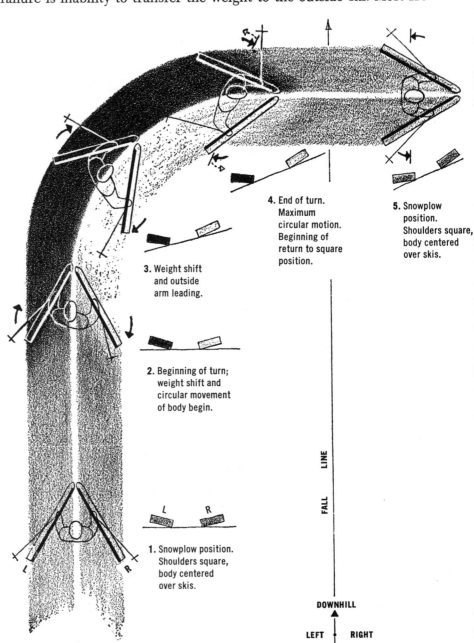

4. End of turn. Maximum circular motion. Beginning of return to square position.

5. Snowplow position. Shoulders square, body centered over skis.

3. Weight shift and outside arm leading.

2. Beginning of turn; weight shift and circular movement of body begin.

1. Snowplow position. Shoulders square, body centered over skis.

FALL LINE

DOWNHILL

LEFT   RIGHT

UPHILL

Figure 33—Snowplow Turn with Weight Shift and Body Motion

Notice that during turn shoulders are at right angles to outside—i.e., down-hill—ski.

1. Snowplow.

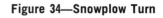

2. Midturn.

Figure 34—Snowplow Turn

3. Turn is completed while "V" position is held.

quently, this is brought about by a mistaken notion that proper weight shift can be accomplished by tilting the pelvis, thus getting the hip over the ski to be weighted. This is absolutely wrong; the hips and shoulders should remain symmetrically centered with respect to the spine. It is the flexed knee which must be placed directly over the ski to be weighted. Another frequent cause of the same failure is a misguided attempt to press the outside ski of the turn into the snow by muscular force, instead of by weighting it, but in pressing a ski into the snow one's body is pushed away from it, so actually the weight will end up over the other ski.

If the weighted ski does not turn, but merely goes straight in the direction it's pointed you are edging it too much. If the inside unweighted ski does not follow around the turn, it is edged too much, most likely because the knee has straightened and stiffened.

Don't jerk your weight over, don't jump onto the ski you want to weight, but gradually get all your weight over in a smooth, fluid motion. It is important to maintain the snowplow throughout the turn, with tips together and the skis and body turning as one unit.

Circular Motion

The next element we introduce into the turn will make it much easier to get around, and a complete and rather nice-looking turn will result. Furthermore, this new element is going to be of great importance later, in the more advanced slow-speed turns and in the high-speed turns. It is called circular motion. It is, in essence, the pivoting of the upper body in the direction you wish to turn.

On your first attempt to use circular motion in the snowplow turn, choose a part of the slope with which you are familiar and on which you have successfully executed turns with weight-shifting alone. Start down in the snowplow position and hold it until you are descending the hill at uniform, fairly slow speed. Start your weight-shifting in the usual way, and as your weight commences to come over the ski which guides the turn, slowly pivot the upper body in the direction of the turn so that the outside shoulder will stay above and at right angles to the outside ski. This movement, which is done slowly over the full length of the turn, is a smooth motion of shoulders and upper body.

Suppose you want to make a right snowplow turn. You are moving down the slope, in full control, at uniform speed, in snowplow position. Start shifting your weight onto your left ski. Simultaneously, begin the pivoting motion of the upper body. Don't jerk around, but coordinate weight shift and body motion smoothly and easily, synchronizing them in such a measured way that the motion is made to last throughout the turn. Maximum pivoting should be achieved at the same instant that the turn is completed, not before.

It is essential, in employing circular motion, to flex the knees, bending into a deeper crouch than that used in the snowplow with which the turn was commenced, making sure that in flexing the knees the seat is not thrust out behind, nor the hips shifted to the outside of the turn. The pivoting and knee action together make one "around-and-down" motion.

Using Lift in the Snowplow Turn

Now comes the final refinement of your snowplow turn. It will make the entire turn easier, neater, and more directly valuable in preparing yourself for the faster turns to come.

Just before you start the simultaneous shifting of weight and circular motion use *lift*, the same lift you learned to use in starting the straight snowplow. This is the final perfection of the snowplow turn from the fall line.

Here is the perfected turn, analyzed step by step: You are coming down the fall line in straight snowplow position. You select the spot where you want to start your turn. As you approach it, *lift*. At the "weightless" moment and just as you are ready to start sinking down again, you simultaneously start your circular motion and weight shift.

As the turn progresses, you continue to sink down and this sinking and the upper-body motion synchronize smoothly. The knees continue to bend as you approach the end of the turn. At the end of the turn, circular motion ceases, and the knees are rather deeply flexed. Don't stop there; this is the point at which the weight comes back on both skis, the body pivots back to normal position, and the knees straighten somewhat so that you return to the same straight snowplow position you started with, but turned ninety degrees from the fall line.

Study the perfected snowplow turn as shown in the drawing, Figure 35. Note especially the position of arms and shoulders, the circular body motion, the weighting of the skis.

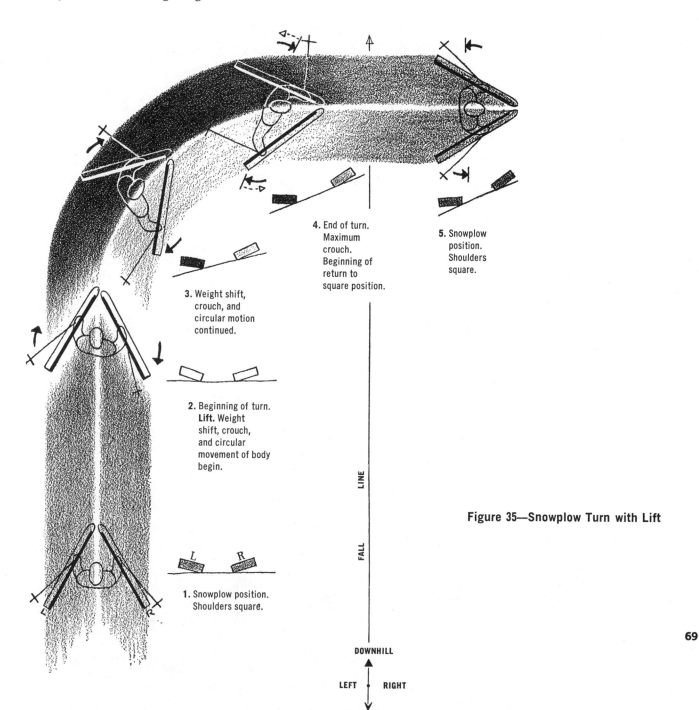

4. End of turn. Maximum crouch. Beginning of return to square position.

5. Snowplow position. Shoulders square.

3. Weight shift, crouch, and circular motion continued.

2. Beginning of turn. **Lift.** Weight shift, crouch, and circular movement of body begin.

1. Snowplow position. Shoulders square.

L   R

FALL LINE

DOWNHILL

LEFT   RIGHT

UPHILL

Figure 35—Snowplow Turn with Lift

The phases of the right turn are: 1. Straight snowplow down the fall line. Shoulders square, weighting and edging of skis equal. 2. Now lift—and weight shift and circular motion commence. Outside (left) ski edged a little more than in 1, inside (right) ski, a little less. 3. Weight has shifted and body motion continues. Skier is still sinking down from lift. 4. End of turn with outside shoulder at right angle to outside ski. Shoulders and knees begin return to normal, symmetrical position. 5. Skier in correct snowplow position with body at right angle to his direction; weight and edging equal on both skis. Figure 36 illustrates, better than words can tell, the most typical snowplow-turn errors.

Figure 36—Snowplow-Turn Errors

1. Skier bent over from waist; ski tips too far apart; knees stiff; downhill shoulder is dropped.

2. Downhill ski pushed ahead; inside knee stiff; inside ski overedged.
SURE RESULTS: Crossed skis, no turn, a fall, frustration, humiliation.
CURE: Get up and try again—at once.

Now you are ready for some fun. You can, by connecting a series of snowplow turns, descend an entire slope in a series of linked S's. This is interesting to do, it is skiing in control, it is far less tiring as a means of maintaining uniform slow speed down a hill than the straight snowplow. It will also render you capable of dealing safely and neatly with steeper, longer hills.

To link snowplow turns, start down your practice hill in snowplow position, execute a snowplow turn (using weight shift, lift, and circular motion) and end it properly with a little deeper crouch than straight downhill position requires, and with your circular motion completely expended. Now, instead of just bringing your shoulders back square and returning to normal stance, you immediately initiate another turn, in the opposite direction. Hold your snowplow position, use your crouch to get good lift for the start of the new turn, and simultaneously start your lift, weight shift, and circular motion. When this second turn is coming to completion, start your third, in the same way that you started your second but, of course, in the new direction.

Using these linked snowplow turns, you can descend the entire slope in a series of turns which cross and recross the fall line. Try to make them in rhythm, as if doing them to music, making the end of one turn and the beginning of the next turn flow together, without visible pause, without jerking. The synchronizing of lift, weight shift, and circular motion—lift, weight shift, and circular motion—is extremely important and worth considerable practice. Notice the easy, fluid quality of the linked turns in Figure 37. Study the diagram and drawing in Figure 38.

Linking snowplow turns thus, you discover something wonderful, a free dividend for all your work and practice. The end phase of your first turn leaves you all set to start your second turn. Having used up, in the first turn, your full circular motion, you are all set to pivot in the opposite direction in the second turn. The end of the first turn is actually a preparation (or countermotion) for the second.

This preparation, or countermotion, is of vital importance in all turns to come. We are going to learn to execute it, intentionally, in unlinked turns, when we come to the advanced snowplow turn. Before we start learning this turn, however, we are going to backtrack to our old friend the traverse. This time, the tired skier will be pleased to learn, we are going to traverse *downhill*, with gravity instead of muscle doing the work.

Linking Snowplow Turns

1

2

3

Figure 37—Linked Snowplow Turns

1. Skier is turning left.
2. Completion of left turn; body is in position for initiating right turn.
3. Midphase of right turn.
4. Completion of right turn; body is in position for initiating linked left turn.

72

4

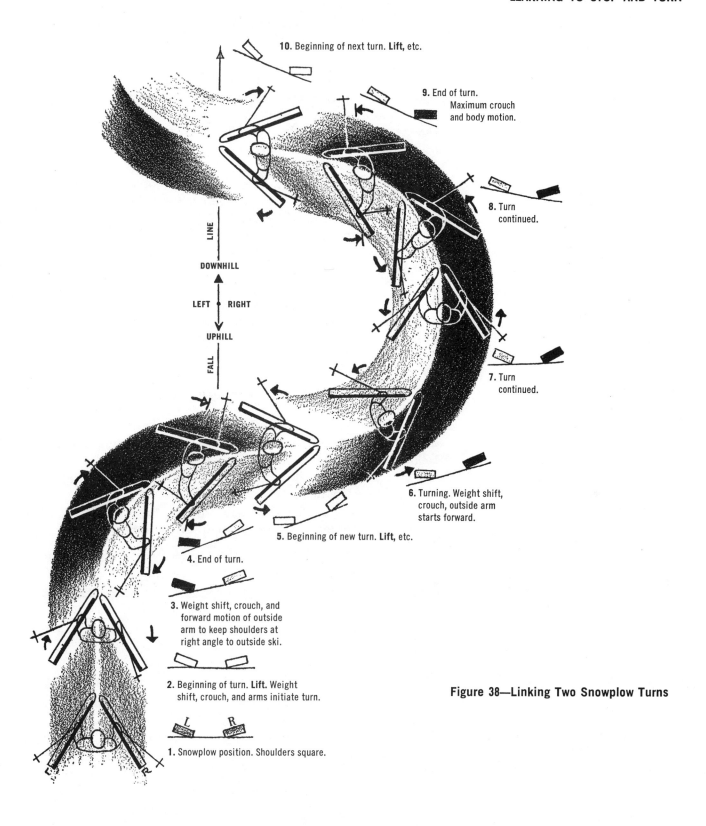

10. Beginning of next turn. **Lift,** etc.

9. End of turn. Maximum crouch and body motion.

8. Turn continued.

7. Turn continued.

LINE
DOWNHILL
LEFT • RIGHT
UPHILL
FALL

6. Turning. Weight shift, crouch, outside arm starts forward.

5. Beginning of new turn. **Lift,** etc.

4. End of turn.

3. Weight shift, crouch, and forward motion of outside arm to keep shoulders at right angle to outside ski.

2. Beginning of turn. **Lift.** Weight shift, crouch, and arms initiate turn.

1. Snowplow position. Shoulders square.

Figure 38—Linking Two Snowplow Turns

Do's and Don'ts

Do snowplow with both skis equally stemmed and equally weighted.

Do put pressure on the heels of the skis to make you come to a stop in the snowplow. Keep your weight centered on your skis.

Do keep arms free of your body and in correct position.

Do lift from the knees, keeping your weight centered, not by shrugging your shoulders.

Do synchronize weight shift, knee action, and circular motion.

Do hold your V, and keep ski tips together throughout the snowplow turn.

Do make your linked turns rhythmical, letting one flow immediately into the next. Hum a tune with a regular beat and link your turns to music.

DON'T plow with one ski. Keep both skis equally edged.

DON'T snowplow on the tips of your skis. You can't press down your heels when you're skiing on your toes.

DON'T press arms to sides—keep your arms free and relaxed for lateral stability.

DON'T try to lift by jumping or straightening the body and knees completely.

DON'T mistake shadow boxing for circular motion; the arms, shoulders and upper body move together in a smooth pivot, not unlike the follow-through in tennis or golf.

DON'T over-pivot; if you do, your weight will come onto the inside ski of your snowplow turn.

DON'T let the turns in your links come around too far; this will slow you to a virtual stop and will destroy your rhythm.

CHAPTER FOUR

DESCENT PLUS CONTROL

By now you should be able to snowplow and snowplow-turn from the fall line with ease, with confidence, and at will. You are ready for steeper hills, then, and you may not want to tackle a new, more abrupt slope for the first time head on, in either snowplow or schuss position. Your method of descent, therefore, will be in a series of downhill traverses. Do you recall the plodding uphill traverses, zigzagging up the hill with kick turns between the zigs and the zags? In traversing downhill, you also zigzag, but it's easier, and in place of the kick turn to change your direction you use the advanced snowplow turn.

Traversing Downhill

For your first traverse, start either at the top of that ideal practice hill we talked about, the one which has a top right where you want it, or start from a standstill partway up the kind of slope you're more apt to be coping with. Before starting down from mid-slope, you stand across the slope—that is, with skis at right angles to the fall line. Brace yourself against sliding with your poles, then step around a little until you're pointing your skis somewhat downhill, at a diagonal between the fall line and the horizontal. Keep your skis parallel and edge them on their uphill edges (toward the slope) as you did in the uphill traverse. Advance the uphill ski a couple of inches. The weight is nearly equal on both skis, although the downhill ski bears a little more of the weight than the uphill ski. (Remember, the greatest stability results from skiing on both skis as much as possible.)*

Now, let go with your poles, and you start to angle across the slope, losing altitude as you go. This crosswise traveling, in which you cover distance laterally while you gradually descend the hill, is called traversing downhill.

Suppose you want to traverse down a hill from its upper left side to its lower right side. The left ski is on its inside edge, the right ski on its outside edge. Skis quite close together. Right ski a bit ahead of left ski. Weight virtually equal on both skis, although the left (downhill) ski

---

* The tendency of beginners who are learning to traverse downhill is to try to hug the slope out of fear of the terrifying void which experts assure them is only a gentle practice slope. This fear leads them to place most of their weight on the uphill ski, a sure way to fall. To overcome this fault, teachers drill their charges in the idea of always weighting the downhill ski. As a result, many beginners have the mistaken notion that they must ski only on the downhill ski, the uphill ski going along just for the ride.

carries a little more weight than the right. An important thing to bear in mind in traversing is that the knees must be limber and pressed very slightly inward, toward the slope. That is the *only* way you can edge comfortably and sufficiently to keep from slipping sideways. But don't lock your knees. That is the most common fault and the most fatal to a proper traverse. (This slight pressing in of the knees, which you'll probably find yourself doing automatically, is a foretaste of "angulation," about which you'll learn more when you get to advanced techniques.)

The body is vertical, with shoulders square and level; you must stand upright on the skis. It is hard to bring yourself to do this, since you instinctively try to hug the slope with your body, but you will soon discover that stability on skis very frequently lies in the direction of thwarting the more chicken instincts. Study the photographs in Figure 39 to see how the experts perform the traverse. You might also profit by looking at the skier in Figure 40. The ski gremlins have overpowered him utterly; he is making all the beginner's mistakes. (Out of finer feeling, we are not showing you the next picture, in which our poor friend is at the bottom of the slope, having made the trip down on

1. From the front.

Figure 39—Downhill Traverse

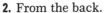

2. From the back.

Figure 40—Wrong Downhill Traverse

1. Knees locked, skis apart.
2. Lower shoulder dropped; skis apart; uphill ski weighted, hips tilted toward the slope.
(Note, in No. 2 particularly, stress and strains in all directions. Besides being unstable, skiing this way is terribly hard work.)

his left side, also his right side, also his back, his stomach, his head, his seat—in fact, everything but his skis. It is a fast way down, but it's unpredictable, tiring, snowy under the ski parka, and it somehow lacks style.)

Edge Control and Sideslipping

Before going on to the more advanced turns (advanced snowplow turn, stem turn and the high-speed turns) we'll take what may seem to be time out to practice a maneuver which is not only advantageous in developing the ability to ski under full control, but which has within it motions of the body and maneuverings of the skis that are essential to further progress and to the ultimate mastering of a complete, modern ski technique. In order to do this, we'll pick a nice smooth slope of good gradient, and preferably packed. Stand across the slope—that is, at right angles to the fall line—with skis close together and parallel, edged into the slope to maintain your position. Upper ski a couple of inches ahead, weight equal on both skis.

You've already learned lift and its advantages in momentarily unweighting the skis. In your standing position assume the crouch which precedes lift; then lift and simultaneously release the edges of the skis so that they proceed down the fall line at right angles to it, remaining parallel and close together, sliding over the snow—sliding down *sideways*. Then go into the crouch position as you edge to stop.

The first time you try this it may be rough and jerky, it may seem hard to keep the skis parallel, and the tips or heels may tend to turn toward the fall line. Very soon, however, you will learn that by shifting your weight forward or back you can keep your course down the fall

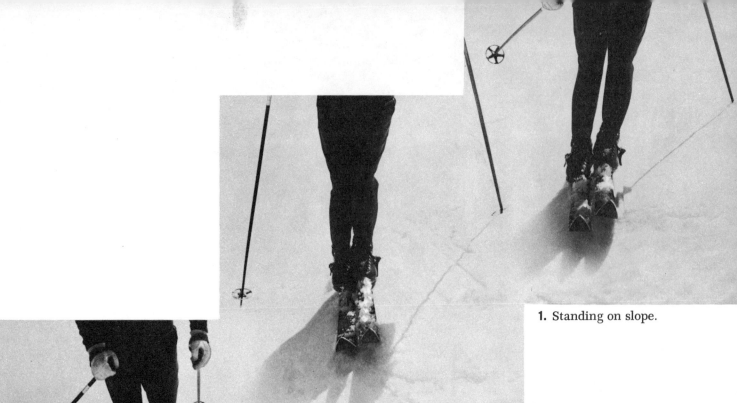

1. Standing on slope.

2. Release edges and sideslip.

Figure 41—Controlled Sideslip

3. Edge to stop. (Note slight angulation.)

line with tips and heels even—that is, at the same altitude—and you will be able to keep the skis together and parallel. See Figures 41 and 42.

Once you have mastered the process of crouch-lift-and-release—sideslip—crouch-and-edge, you are ready to do a series of sideslips in rhythmic motion, in which the crouch that commences a slip and the crouch that terminates it (with the edges biting in) lead smoothly into each other in a progression which might be described thus: crouch, lift and release edges, crouch and edge, lift and release edges, crouch and edge, etc., with sideslips between each pair of crouches.

When you have learned to do this rhythmically, smoothly, easily, you are not only ready to learn the advanced snowplow turn, but you have gone a long way toward perfecting a type of body, ski and edge

Figure 42—Sideslip in Profile

1. Skier slightly crouched, skis sharply edged into slope.

2. Lift and release edges to initiate slip.

3. Crouch and edge sharply to stop.

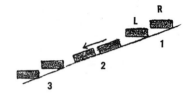

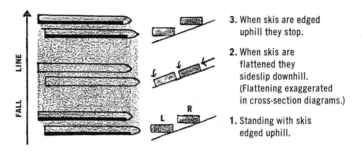

3. When skis are edged
uphill they stop.

2. When skis are
flattened they
sideslip downhill.
(Flattening exaggerated
in cross-section diagrams.)

1. Standing with skis
edged uphill.

Figure 43—Controlled Sideslip

control that will be invaluable to you as you go on into advanced technique.

A few important pointers will make your mastery of the controlled sideslip easier. First, refer to Figure 23 again to see how releasing the edges too much may result in your catching the downhill edges and falling. Although the released edges bring the surface of the ski virtually flat to the snow, there should still be a slight amount of edging, just enough to keep the downhill edges from coming into contact with the surface of the snow and possibly catching, to throw you into a spill. Another important point to remember is that the releasing of the edges should not be accomplished by holding the feet and ankles rigid and releasing only from the knees. Knees *and* ankles, with emphasis on the ankles, are the parts of the body that come into play in releasing the edges and in re-edging to stop. Finally, although the prime requisite of all good skiing is to ski on both skis equally, as much as possible and whenever possible, in this kind of controlled sideslipping in which one edges to a stop it will be easier to make the stop clean and the edging precise if the downhill ski bears a bit more weight than the uphill ski at the time of edging.

Advanced Snowplow Turn

The advanced snowplow turn differs from the snowplow turn in four major respects. First, it is done from a traverse and toward the fall line, instead of away from the fall line. Second, preparation (i.e., countermotion) is employed in the starting of the turn. Third, the turn is almost 180 degrees instead of 90 degrees; that is, one turns from a traverse in one direction all the way around to a traverse in the opposite direction. (The snowplow turn, you will recall, turns only 90 degrees away from the fall line.) Fourth, the skis are allowed to run together—parallel—at the completion of the turn.

Now we must consider the matter of preparation, or countermotion (which we discovered in linked snowplow turns) and its correct execution, and then we can get on to the advanced snowplow turn itself.

Let us observe, for a moment, a few other sports.

You know how a baseball batter swings the bat back before smashing at the ball? How a tennis player takes back his racket before making a forehand drive? How a golfer swings the club back before lacing into the ball to send it on its way in a long drive? In skiing, this windup, this act of getting set and giving yourself room and momentum for your circular body motion, is called "preparation" or "countermotion" or "counterpivot."

How do you use it to precede the actual turning in the advanced snowplow turn? It's easy. In a right turn from a traverse to the left, you want to pivot your body to the right. Before doing so, get prepared with a slight countermotion of the upper body. Now, when you start your weight shift to the left ski, and your circular motion to the right, you'll have plenty of room in which to pivot throughout the turn. The position—or rather the motion—of hands and arms is important, too. In proper preparation the uphill arm and hand turn with the uphill shoulder, so that in maximum preparation the uphill hand is directly over the rear part of the ski. Similarly, the downhill hand moves around and forward.

Now that you understand preparation for a turn, and know how to use circular motion, you are ready for the advanced snowplow turn.

Start traversing down the practice hill. Traverse at least thirty feet. Lift a little, to help get the skis into snowplow position. Hold the snowplow for at least fifteen feet, then counterpivot and at the same time sink a little lower down, remembering not to squat, but to flex knees and ankles. Now, simultaneously, start lift, start circular motion, start weight shift—in other words, start turning toward the fall line. Just before the turn comes full around—that is, when you are at the desired traversing angle in the opposite direction from your original traverse—let the skis run together, close and parallel, and as they do so, bring the shoulders back square and advance the inside (uphill) ski of the turn a couple of inches.

Traverse now in the new direction, again for at least thirty feet, then snowplow, advanced-snowplow-turn, and again traverse. Continue in this way until you get down the slope in a series of traverses joined by advanced snowplow turns. Do this many times, until you can start in either direction, traverse in either direction, turn from a traverse in either direction, all with equal ease and with a sense of mastery and freedom from anxiety.

Figure 44—Advanced Snowplow Turn from the Rear Analyzed

1. Traverse.
2. Slight crouch in preparation for lift.
3. Lift and plow.
4. Body preparation for circular motion.
5. Slight lift and circular motion to bring shoulders at right angles to outside (left and downhill) ski.
6. End phase of turn, skis running together into parallel, traverse position.
7. Traverse in new direction.

Figure 44 is a step-by-step picture of one advanced snowplow turn.

Here are the steps in a right turn, as they are shown in Figures 44, 45, and 46, analyzed one by one. Remember, they are not executed in steps, but in flowing, synchronized movements; the step-by-step analysis can only stop the action for you at various phases of the maneuver, so that you may better understand what happens and when.

1. TRAVERSE: Skier is in traverse from upper right of the hill toward lower left. Shoulders square, weight on both skis (although the right ski carries a very little more weight than the left). Left ski is leading right by one or two inches. Knees are slightly angulated toward slope.
2. CROUCH: Skier crouches slightly, and . . .
3. LIFT AND SNOWPLOW: Lift is employed in order to make an easy snowplow.
4. PREPARATION: Snowplow position is held while skier counter-pivots shoulders and simultaneously crouches a little more than normal traverse position requires. Both skis are still on inner edges, as in straight snowplow.
5. CIRCULAR MOTION: Lift, weight shift, and pivoting of upper body commence simultaneously.
6. IN FALL LINE: In the fall line, circular motion has progressed to halfway point and shoulders are now in symmetrical snowplow position. Sinking into crouch, which commenced as weight went onto left ski, continues. Right ski is flattening (in preparation for edging on right edge).
7. ACROSS FALL LINE: Circular motion is almost completed.
8. COMPLETION OF BODY MOTION AND CROUCH: Turn is accomplished.
9. STRAIGHTENING: As skier starts to rise from crouch, right ski begins going over onto its uphill edge and skis begin closing (running together). At the same time, circular motion is neutralized as body and shoulders come squarely over parallel skis.
10. TRAVERSE: Traverse again. Skis parallel and close together, right ski has come into the lead, weight nearly equal, shoulders square, normal bend of knees and slight angulation, both skis on uphill edges.

Once you have mastered traversing and the advanced snowplow turn, you are ready for a refresher demonstration of your skill, either to test yourself or to show off to admiring novices—*because you are no longer a novice!*

Want to prove it? Put on your skis, walk to the practice slope, start up in traverses with kick turns between them. When the hill gets steeper, shift to the half side step, and when the going gets tiresome that way, or if the width of the hill narrows, switch to herringbone.

Figure 45—Advanced Snowplow Turn with Skier Approaching Camera and Turning Away to the Left

1. Traverse.
2. Lift and snowplow.
3. Preparation and countermotion.
4. Lift and circular motion, outside hand leading shoulder square to outside ski.
5. Completion of turn.
6. Skis running together, uphill ski moving ahead.

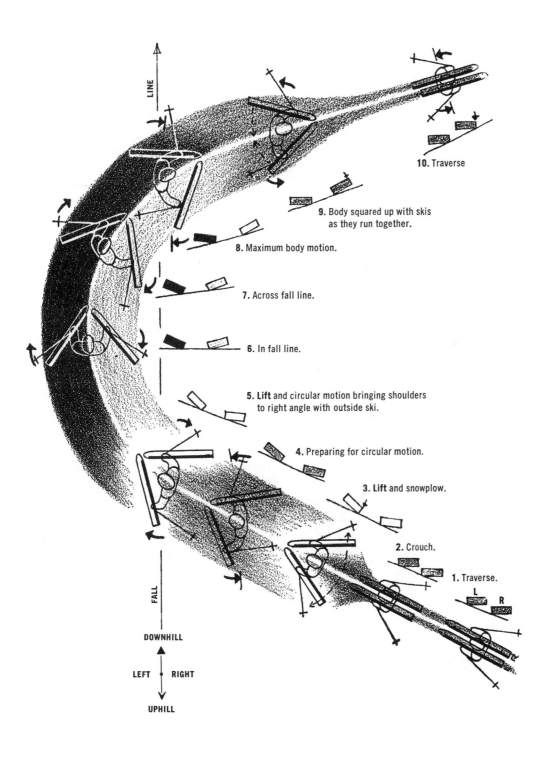

10. Traverse

9. Body squared up with skis as they run together.

8. Maximum body motion.

7. Across fall line.

6. In fall line.

5. Lift and circular motion bringing shoulders to right angle with outside ski.

4. Preparing for circular motion.

3. Lift and snowplow.

2. Crouch.

1. Traverse.

L   R

LINE

FALL

DOWNHILL

LEFT   RIGHT

UPHILL

Figure 46—Advanced Snowplow Turn

Use the full side step for the final ascent. Start down the fall line in a schuss, snowplow, link a few snowplow turns, traverse, advanced-snowplow-turn, traverse again, advanced-snowplow-turn, traverse to the center of the slope, then snowplow-turn into fall line, come down a way at constant speed in snowplow position, then let skis run together and schuss the rest of the slope, stopping with a snowplow on the level.

Nice going! But you're even better than you realize. Those advanced snowplow turns between traverses are very closely related to stem turns. And you're ready to learn the stem turn now. But that isn't all. By virtue of having learned the right way, you can now look back, not too far, to first steps on skis and realize that from now on everything is largely a matter of refinements and improving technique. The fundamentals are already learned and behind you—or, rather, with you, for you'll use them all the time. There has been no waste motion.

Do's and Don'ts

Do, in traversing, keep skis close together and parallel, with (important) the uphill ski always a little ahead.

Do, in traverse, employ equal edging and virtually equal weighting.

Do stay in the snowplow long enough to get completely set, when turning from a traverse.

Do come into a full traverse, with skis together, before starting a new turn.

DON'T lean toward the hill when traversing.

DON'T drop either shoulder.

DON'T try to brake speed in a traverse with the edge of your uphill ski.

DON'T let the skis run together until you are sufficiently far around in your turn for the next traverse.

DON'T push the outside ski of your turns ahead too far. If you do, the inside knee will straighten, and the skis won't run together easily at the end of the turn.

DON'T distort your posture by overdoing slight, natural angulation.

CHAPTER FIVE

THE STEM TURN AND THE PRE-CHRISTIANIA

The stem turn differs from the advanced snowplow turn in two principal respects: (1) It is made at higher speed (i.e., the traverse from which it is made is closer to the fall line); and (2) the skis, instead of being stemmed (that is, pressed out at the heels into the snowplow) simultaneously, are stemmed separately, first the downhill ski, then the uphill ski.

There is a critical difference which distinguishes this stemming from the snowplow, however: the alternate stemming of the downhill and uphill skis is not employed to reduce speed, as in the snowplow, but as preparation for the turn itself.

Let us pause to say a bit about this matter of preparation, as we have done in the past with other terms that apply to actions not yet accomplished at high speed, but which are important to learn at comparatively slow speeds. The kind of preparation for a turn is achieved by the alternate stemming of the skis in the stem turn and is actually intended to create a platform from which the turn itself is launched. This platform will be of great importance in later, high-speed turns; in the stem turn it can be learned in slow motion and—as with all rapid actions that are learned slowly—it will automatically become modified as speed and confidence increase.

There is another new term to be introduced here, known as the "hook." You will learn all about it later, but right now it seems worth pointing out that the manner of stemming the skis in the stem turn is analogous to a two-ski hook. Don't worry about the word "hook" now; just keep it in mind for later. All you need to know about the hook for now is that it is, essentially, a short, brief—almost instantaneous— and vigorous stemming, with sharp edging of *both* skis in the same direction and parallel, combined with automatic and natural angulation.

Before actually describing the phases of the stem turn, we'd like to stress once more that the need for proper preparation of turns is not to be thought of as getting frozen into a fixed posture. The fact is that proper preparation induces the exact opposite, that is, flow, fluency, even a kind of looseness. Again, we can turn to analogies in other sports. Preparation for ski maneuvers is quite comparable to the body positioning employed by a tennis player just before executing a fore-hand or backhand drive. Golfers, too, prepare for wielding the club by proper body positioning. To continue the analogy: The moment the club or racket contacts the ball is the equivalent of a skiing turn itself, and there is a follow-through which is the equivalent of completing the ski turn with grace, instead of jerkiness induced by abrupt interruption of motion and consequent strain on leg muscles. In fact, one of our major quarrels with some of the current fads in skiing is that the maneuvers are so artificial, i.e., not natural to fluidity of body motion, that the skier becomes frozen into an unnatural position and maintains it rigidly throughout the turn, thus depriving himself of the control that is only possible with free, easy, natural movement of the body and the consequent lightness and agility that a skier requires. The preliminary stemming of the downhill ski in the stem turn becomes absolutely essential in the development of high-speed turns and wedeln. But let us repeat to the point of sounding obsessed: The preliminary stemming is not a brake on speed, it is a movement that naturally places the body in the correct position for performing the turn smoothly and gracefully, carving it, rather than forcing it—with consequent undesirable slipping.

Stem Turn

The following is an analysis of a stem turn to the right.

1. Skier is in a traverse, from upper right of hill toward lower left. The traverse is steeper (closer to the fall line) than any previously used, and the skier has more speed as a result.
2. Simultaneously, countermotion and stemming of right (downhill) ski.
3. Weight is carried now on stemmed right ski while left ski is stemmed.
4. As left ski attains full stem position, skier lifts, and starts circular motion to the right and weight shift to left ski.
5. Ski tips are kept close together (by maintaining outward pressure on heels) as skier approaches fall line. In the fall line the skis and body and shoulders are in symmetrical, snowplow position, although weight is on left ski.
6. As fall line is passed, and circular motion continues, the right ski is allowed to run together with the left. As the turn finishes in the new traverse the right ski goes over onto its uphill edge and the skis come parallel and close together, with right ski in the lead.

Throughout the turn, hands and arms move freely and naturally with the shoulders, as in the snowplow turns.

You may have noticed that the stemming of the downhill ski (the ski on the inside of the turn) is sometimes difficult, especially if the snow is deep enough to offer resistance to the sideward pushing out of the heel. In addition, the act of stemming this ski may reduce the necessary speed for making a nice smooth turn. This is easily overcome.

The skier is in traverse, weight virtually equal on both skis. He selects the point at which he wants to commence his turn. As he approaches it, he crouches down a little. He then lifts. At the moment when the highest elevation of the lift is reached, both skis are somewhat unweighted. Now, as the sinking down after the lift commences, the returning body weight is taken up on the outside (uphill) ski, and simultaneously countermotion is begun. As this preparation approaches completion the weight is brought onto the stemmed downhill ski, so that in the crouch at the end of the sinking-down movement the preparation is completed, and the uphill ski is relieved of weight. This is the favorable time to stem the uphill ski. When it is sufficiently stemmed the skier simultaneously starts the rising phase of another lift and circular motion. He then executes the balance of the turn in the usual way, using the around-and-down movement which is a combination of circular motion and sinking from the lift into the crouch.

The explanation of the foregoing sounds extremely complicated. Actually, it is a very simple matter, once understood, and is done with even and smooth-flowing motion, in which the various movements, separately described, are all integral parts of one continuous movement.

Here is a step-by-step analysis and description (Figures 47, 48 and 49).

1. TRAVERSE: Steeper and faster than in previous traverses.
2. CROUCH: Bend forward from knees, *seat pulled in. Don't sit.*
3. LIFT: Both skis "weightless."
4. COUNTERMOTION: At the end of lifting, weight comes down on uphill ski. Start of sinking down in crouch is accompanied by start of slight stemming of lower ski, and preparation for circular motion.
5. STEM: At the end of countermotion, weight comes full on stemmed (downhill) ski. The outside, uphill ski is now nearly weightless and is stemmed. The downhill ski is already stemmed, and the body is ready for lift.
6. LIFT.
7. WEIGHT SHIFT AND CIRCULAR MOTION: The instant when highest elevation in the lift is achieved and the sinking down is about to begin, body pivot and weight shift to uphill (outside) ski are also begun.
8. FALL LINE: Circular motion has progressed to halfway point, so that in the fall line the skier is in straight snowplow position, but with the weight already full on the outside ski.
9. START OF CLOSE: As skier crosses the fall line and as the outside ski of the turn comes into line with the intended traverse in the new direction, the skis start to close, the inside ski coming parallel

with the outside ski and moving ahead into the lead as it does so. The edging of this ski simultaneously changes to the uphill edge. Meanwhile, full crouch and full circular motion have been achieved, so that as the skis start to close, the skier rises to normal posture for the traverse and shoulders come square over the skis again.

10. TRAVERSE IN NEW DIRECTION.

Study the photographs of the stem turn carefully, noting skis, hands, poles, ankles, knees, body, shoulders—and the changing of the edging on the inside ski of the turn. Note, too, the path carved by the skis.

Figure 47—Stem Turn from Traverse Approaching Camera and Turning Away to the Left

1. Traverse.
2. Stem lower ski and prepare for circular motion.
3. Ready to lift.
4. Lift and commence circular motion of body.
5. Midturn; shoulders are at right angles to outside ski.
6. Let skis begin running together again.
7. Traverse, skis parallel, body position normal.

Figure 48—Stem Turn Seen from the Rear

It is important to practice stem turns on different hills, at different speeds, from traverses of various angles. Learn to make a smooth descent of hills which are not too steep, placing your stem turns and traverses where you want them. You will discover that the degree of stemming of the lower ski depends on the steepness of the slope and the depth of the snow, and you will accustom yourself to gauging your requirements. The degree of stemming and the amount of lift are also influenced by the speed at which the turn is entered.

Don't attempt to link stem turns; they are meant for joining traverses. Don't hold your snowplow position, in which both skis are stemmed; as soon as the uphill ski is in position, go right into your turn.

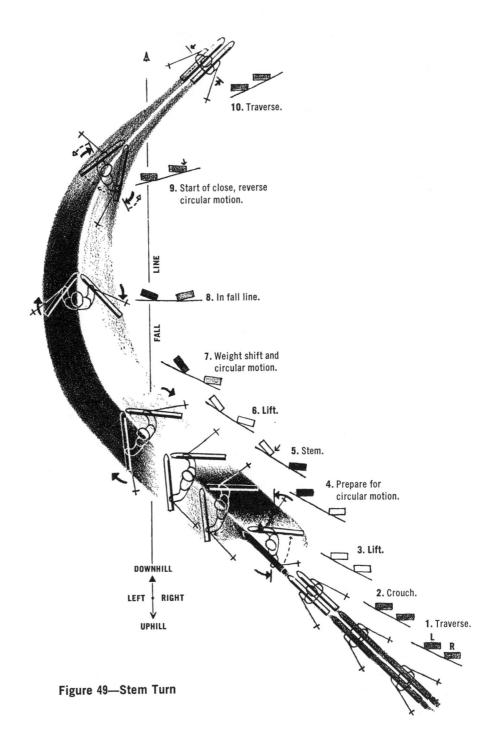

10. Traverse.

9. Start of close, reverse
circular motion.

8. In fall line.

7. Weight shift and
circular motion.

6. Lift.

5. Stem.

4. Prepare for
circular motion.

3. Lift.

2. Crouch.

1. Traverse.

L R

DOWNHILL

LEFT   RIGHT

UPHILL

Figure 49—Stem Turn

Figure 50—Wrong Starting of Stem Turn

The position (corresponding to No. 2 in Figure 47) is so bad as to doom the entire turn. The stiff lower knee has thrown the weight on the uphill ski, and the skier has leaned in toward the slope. In addition, the stance is too erect and rigid.

The pre-christiania differs from the stem turn in one major respect. The skis, instead of being allowed to run together by themselves, are intentionally closed; that is, the inside ski of the turn is drawn parallel with, close to, and a little ahead of the outside ski. In order to accomplish this with finesse and ease on packed slopes, and without undue muscular strain in deeper snow, lift is used to relieve the pressure of the body's weight on the skis.

The pre-christiania is done at moderately good speed, and it requires good circular motion to overcome centrifugal pull in the turn, and the pull of gravity along the fall line. The first phases of the turn are similar to those for the stem turn, and the position in the fall line is again instantaneously a symmetrical snowplow with the weight on the outside ski. Speed is a little greater, lift a bit more pronounced, the crouch toward the end of the turn a little deeper. As the outside ski comes into the direction of the new traverse, the skier simultaneously

Pre-Christiania

starts the following three motions: (1) lift; (2) turning of the inside ski of the turn onto its outside (uphill) edge; and (3) drawing of the inside ski parallel, close to, and into the lead of the outside ski. The turn ends with body returned to normal traverse position, shoulders square, both skis on their uphill edges and parallel, the uphill ski leading the downhill ski by a few inches, and the weight equal on both skis.

The degree of stemming of the downhill and uphill skis, particularly the latter, depends on speed, obliquity of the traverse, quality of snow. The correct amount of stemming cannot be taught; it is a matter of "feel," which is developed automatically through practice.

A properly executed pre-christie is shown in Figures 51 and 52. Study these photographs and also the diagram in Figure 53. When you have learned to adjust the timing and synchronization of movements in the pre-christie to suit various slopes and speeds, and have learned the fairly rapid closing of the skis after the fall line is passed, it's time

Figure 51—The Pre-Christiania

1. Traverse and body preparation.
2. Stem.
3. Circular motion initiates the turn.
4. As turn continues, crouch to prepare for lift.
5. Lift, then sideslip inside ski toward parallel position.
6. End phase of the pre-christiania with the skis parallel.

Figure 52—Pre-Christiania from the Front, Showing Crucial Phases Where Lift Is Employed to Carve a Smooth Turn and Permit Easy Running of the Skis Together

to get out the family movie camera and take a picture of yourself coming down a slope in linked traverses. You'll be proud of those pictures and so will we.

This turn can be tricky to master in the end phases, where the skis must be closed, lift must be right, and the inside ski changes its edge, but once you learn it you will have entered the door to the most exciting family of turns in all skiing, the true christianias. There's magic in the name, and magical is the sensation of doing them. Magical, too, will be the way you look on skis when you've mastered the christies.

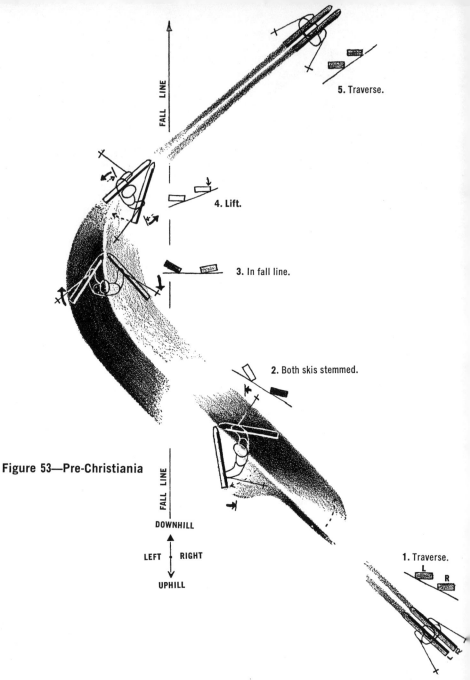

5. Traverse.

FALL LINE

4. Lift.

3. In fall line.

2. Both skis stemmed.

Figure 53—Pre-Christiania

FALL LINE

DOWNHILL

LEFT • RIGHT

UPHILL

1. Traverse.

L

R

Do's and Don'ts   Do be sure to stem with the heels of the skis, not with the entire ski.

Do let the weight come onto the stemmed lower ski before attempting to stem the upper.

Do time the closing of your skis to start when the outside ski comes into the direction of the new traverse.

Do use lift to facilitate the sliding in of the inside ski at the end of the turn.

Do remember to bring the inside ski ahead as the skis close.

Don't, in stemming, let the tips of the skis open.

Don't turn before both skis are in proper stemmed position.

Don't let your skis close too soon; you will stop turning and your new traverse will be steeper than you wish.

Don't lift the inside ski from the snow while closing the skis—it must *slide* parallel to the outside ski.

CHAPTER SIX

EXERCISES AND CONTROLLED SIDESLIPPING

Choose a fairly well-packed and even slope, steep enough, yet one on which you can schuss in comfort. Your object is to schuss the full length of the slope while rising and crouching, up and down, on your skis in a continuous, smooth and cadenced manner. From your correct schuss posture (weight equalized fore and aft, heels down on skis, knees limber, body at right angles to the slope, hips pulled in and skis and shins making an acute angle), rise slowly to an almost completely erect stance by straightening up *without shifting the weight back or forward.* As soon as you are nearly erect (body is not straight; there is still enough bend at ankles, knees, and hips to preserve the loose-jointed springiness which is essential to balance), crouch down slowly, a little farther than normal schuss position requires, and then rise again to full lift position. Continue this up-down-up-down exercise for the length of the practice slope. Keep in mind that in both rise and crouch your weight must remain centered on your skis, your center of gravity maintained exactly between forward and backward leaning, and don't let the heels leave the skis (Figure 54). Lifting the shoulders alone is *not* lifting, it is shrugging.

Lifting

1. Normal position.

Figure 54—Lifting Exercises

2. Crouch.

3. Lift.

Changing Lead   Here is another good security exercise. Schuss down your slope and while doing so lead with first one ski, then the other. Suppose you start down the hill with your left ski a little in the lead of your right. Once you get going, shift your weight onto your left ski (not by swaying the upper body to the left side, nor by shifting the hips) and then slide the right ski about three inches ahead of it. Now shift your weight to the right ski, and slide the left up ahead of it. Keep alternating leads this way for the length of the slope. In changing from one lead to another, don't try to pull the lead ski back. This will stiffen the knees. Leave it where it is, and slide the other ahead of it (Figure 55).

Controlled Sideslipping   The main characteristics of the faster christies are that the skis are parallel (not stemmed) and that they skid in turning. This skidding is an intentional, controlled matter. When forward motion, circular motion and skid are combined, you get a nicely carved turn. And the skid part of the turn, alone, is the sideways slipping we avoided in the traverse by edging our skis on their uphill edges.

In order to learn how the skid works, and how it can be controlled, security exercises called "controlled sideslipping" are very helpful. They are *not* easy, so be kind and patient with yourself.

Figure 55—Changing Lead Ski

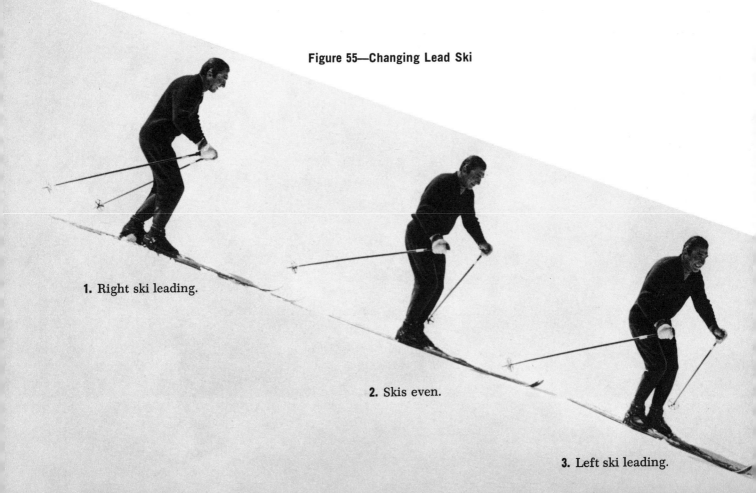

1. Right ski leading.

2. Skis even.

3. Left ski leading.

1. Traverse.

2. Sideslip.

3. Traverse.

Figure 56—Sideslip from Traverse

Start downhill in a traverse, and gradually release (unedge) the skis somewhat. You will continue in the direction of the traverse, but you will also lose altitude by sideslipping. You can alter the amount of slip by increasing or decreasing edging. Increase edging enough, and you will traverse again. You should have such good edge control that you can maintain a uniform rate of slip as you traverse the slope. Don't curve the spine by swaying sideways from the hips, and don't lean into the hill or out from it with the upper body. Keep weight equal on both skis; don't let them slide apart or get out of parallel position (Figures 56 and 57). Descend the slope with alternate slips and traverses until you can do so with ease, slipping and traversing where you want to, calling your shots.

Traversing Slip

Figure 57—Sideslip from Traverse

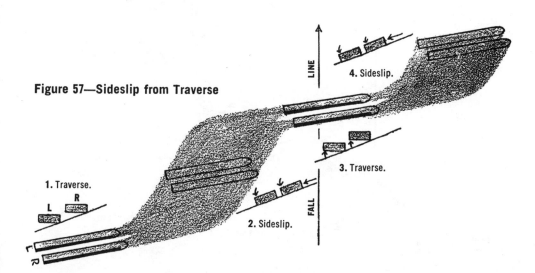

1. Traverse.
L   R

2. Sideslip.

3. Traverse.

4. Sideslip.

LINE

FALL

Sideslipping to Stop

Here is a doubly useful exercise. Not only does it help make you master of your skis for the better learning of the christies, but it provides you with the means of stopping in a fairly fast traverse, for which the snowplow is entirely unsuitable. It makes use of sideslip, countermotion (preparation), lift and circular motion. The skis are kept parallel throughout the maneuver, and the object is to turn rapidly from a traverse to a standstill in a position where the skis are squarely across the slope, not pointing downhill, nor uphill.

Start on your traverse at fair speed. When you are going along nicely, simultaneously crouch and countermove the upper body away from the slope. Don't pause; simultaneously lift with good elevation and pivot toward the slope with rapidity and force. Keep the skis parallel. You will make a sharp, abrupt turn toward the slope. As you come around, sink down fairly deeply from the lift, on flexed and limber knees, edge gradually more to stop sideslipping, meanwhile bringing shoulders back square over the skis.

To make these rapid, "tight" stop turns effectively, you must have good and fast elevation in the lift, enough virtually to unweight both skis. Good elevation does not mean rising upright; it does not mean jerking up, or jumping. It does mean exact timing and fluent, synchronized action of the entire body.

With a little courage and practice, you can make this stop turn from steeper traverses, learning to gauge the edging and the skid and the amount of circular motion required to bring you around so that you are directly across the slope and stopped (Figures 58 and 59).

If your weight is too far forward as you turn, the turn won't come around; if your weight is back too far, the tails of the skis will sail on down the slope, taking you with them, backward, en route to the inevitable dunking. As in every maneuver described in this book, the weight must be kept centered on the skis, so that the skier can instantly adjust to unevenness in snow or terrain by moving his weight in either direction.

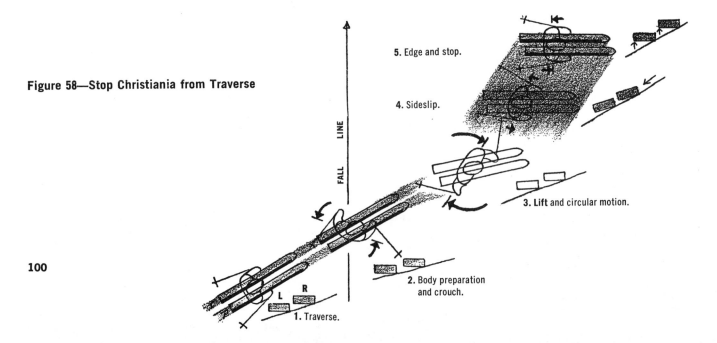

Figure 58—Stop Christiania from Traverse

FALL LINE

5. Edge and stop.

4. Sideslip.

3. **Lift** and circular motion.

2. Body preparation and crouch.

L   R

1. Traverse.

100

Figure 59—Stop Christiania from Traverse

1. Traverse.
2. Lift and start circular motion.
3. Circular motion, heels of skis slide in tightly carved turn.
4. Edge and complete circular motion.
5. Skier has come to a stop. (Note slight natural angulation in **4** and **5**.)

The skier, having come thus far, may well be ready for the adventure of the christiania turns. He *is* ready, provided what has gone before—the snowplow, the snowplow turns, the stem turns, and controlled sideslipping—are all thoroughly mastered and understood. Just to make sure, let's refresh our minds by going back a little and in doing so bring out some hints and ideas which may help us to get stubborn problems cleared up.

Let's think, for a moment, of a corkscrew. Suppose its point is inserted into a cork and we wish to twist it down and all the way in. Since the corkscrew's motion is clockwise, like that of a screw, we move our hand *counterclockwise* before grasping the handle to give it the clockwise twist. We make this counterclockwise motion so that we will have the full turning radius of the wrist to expend in the clockwise motion. We then can drive the corkscrew around and down (Figure 60).

The analogy with a ski turn is, by now, clear. The counterclockwise motion is the countermotion; the screw-wise motion around and down is the body-and-shoulder circular motion combined with the sinking down of the body into a crouch.

Unfortunately, the analogy of the corkscrew is not complete; it takes more than lift, crouch, and circular motion to make skis turn smoothly, fully, and well. This is because the corkscrew is *curved*, whereas skis are straight. To make skis carve a curve at speed, the skier must skid them around the turn. And to achieve this skid, we must recall the controlled sideslips and employ their principles.

Figure 60—The "Corkscrew" Analogy

Hand approaches straight (traverse), then turns counterclockwise in order to get prepared, then turns corkscrew around and down.

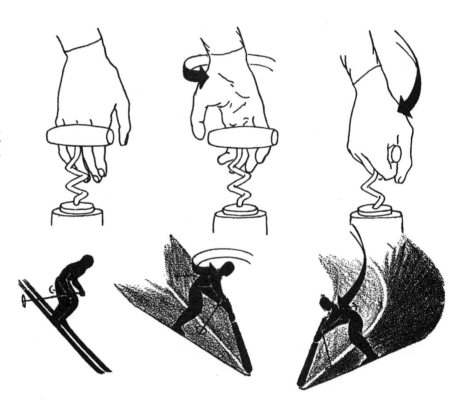

Teetotalers may use the analogy of a screw being driven into a block of wood.

Do's and Don'ts

Do try to keep the skis parallel and close together during the sideslip.

Do keep your shoulders square during the sideslip.

Do keep your weight above your skis, not leaning toward the slope.

Do use lift and circular motion to stop your traverse by turning toward the slope.

Do edge both skis equally toward the hill in the turn from a traverse.

DON'T release edges of the skis completely in sideslipping. If you do, the downhill edges may catch on the snow and spill you.

DON'T let the skis open at the tips or cross at the tails while you sideslip.

DON'T attempt the straight sideslip in deep or soft snow—it is for packed slopes.

DON'T attempt the turn toward the hill from a traverse by twitching your hips or wagging your backside.

DON'T jump around; the skis must stay on the snow throughout the turn toward the slope.

CHAPTER SEVEN

THE BASIC CHRISTIANIA

If you have been combining diligence in learning with the fun of skiing, and have mastered the maneuvers so far explained, you are more than ready for the first of the christies, the basic christie.

The basic christie differs from the stem turn in three major respects: (1) The uphill ski does not stem at all; (2) you must have good speed before going into the turn—at least fifteen miles per hour, if you know how to judge speed; and (3) the skis close parallel much sooner in the basic christie than in the stem turns. Less important differences are: the stemming of the downhill ski is less pronounced than in the stem turn; lift must be good enough to relieve both skis of weight sufficiently so that they can go into the turn readily; the radius of the turn is longer than that of the stem turn; the degree of preparation with the downhill ski and the length of time it lasts are sufficiently diminished so that speed is not checked; the body banks toward the inside of the turn—actually toward the imaginary center of it—and lift plus body motion accomplish most of the work of turning.

All this sounds complicated and like much too much to bear in mind at once—and it is. Try to understand it, and to grasp the mechanics of the turn as they are explained and analyzed, but don't try to remember all the details. If you do, your mind will be so intent on remembering, and so cluttered with fine points of technique, that, likely as not, you'll find yourself having unwittingly executed the "tree christie," an uncomfortable maneuver of very tangible effectiveness, in which you wrap yourself and skis around the nearest tree. While this is indubitably an effective means for stopping, it is not considered good form by ski stylists.

So, don't try to remember everything but do try to understand. Then go out on the slope, and after your half-hour warmup in the snowplow turns (yes, that half-hour warmup is a very good thing for everyone, novice and expert), start doing fast stem turns. Do them on a fairly steep slope, carving curves near the fall line rather than wide turns, with good speed, plenty of body action, good edge control—and you'll find them becoming very nearly basic christies. It takes a sharp eye indeed to tell the difference between a well-executed, fairly fast stem turn and a comparatively slow basic christie. The fact that the uphill ski is not stemmed is the distinguishing mark.

The following analysis of the basic christie, step by step, should be read with constant reference to the photographs and diagrams in Figures 61, 62 and 63.

TRAVERSE: You are coming down the hill at good speed, in a rather steep traverse. (Let us assume you are moving from the upper righthand side of the hill toward the lower left. Downhill is to your right, and you are going to make a right turn across the fall line.) Your left (uphill) ski is very slightly ahead of your right (downhill) ski. Both skis are on their uphill edges.

COUNTERMOTION: Preparation of upper body is executed simultaneously with stemming of the right (downhill) ski, and the crouch preparatory to lift.

START OF TURN: The preparation position is not held. Immediately you are set for the turn; lift, circular motion, weight shift, and edging (on its inside edge) of the left (uphill) ski are initiated. These movements must be executed with sufficient force to start the uphill ski turning, which is accomplished by a lift that is forceful enough to constitute a push-off.

TURNING: Once the turn has commenced and the weight is on the left ski, the skier draws the right (stemmed) ski parallel with the left ski and, while doing so, changes its edge. As the turn progresses, the skis are parallel, both on their right edges, the skier's body is leaning toward the center of the turn, he is sinking down into the crouch which follows his lift, the right ski has moved a little ahead of the left ski, body is continuing smoothly, and hands and arms are moving freely and fully with the shoulders.

END PHASE OF TURN: Just before the skier comes directly into the line of the new traverse, he is crouched, he has fully completed his circular motion, he is skidding somewhat downhill (but if his edging is correct he will not skid much—remember controlled sideslipping?), and his body is leaning in toward the hill enough to counteract centrifugal pull, and enough to prevent edging the skis by bending the ankles, which would be a terrific strain on them. Again, let us stress that a line drawn through the body from head to foot is, if the turn is being done correctly, at right angles to the skis (looking at the skier from front or back). Similarly, looking at the turn from the side, a line drawn through the skier's center of gravity is at right angles to the skis.

TRAVERSE: As the skier comes into the traverse, he can either straighten body and shoulders, continuing in the traverse, or he can use his crouched, prepared position to start a new basic christie in the opposite direction, thereby linking the second turn to the first.

The above is a description of *one* basic christie. No two are exactly

Figure 61—Basic Christiania

Basic Christiania Analyzed

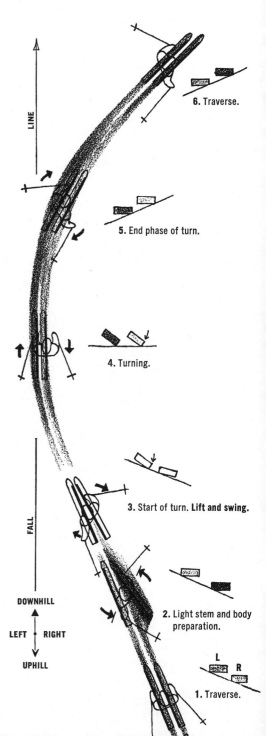

6. Traverse.

5. End phase of turn.

4. Turning.

3. Start of turn. **Lift and swing.**

2. **Light stem and body preparation.**

L R

1. Traverse.

LINE

FALL

DOWNHILL

LEFT | RIGHT

UPHILL

Figure 62—Basic Christiania from the Front

1. Body preparation.
2. Crouch and light stem.
3. Lift and turn, applying circular motion.
4. End phase of basic christiania.

alike. The crucial timing of circular body motion, weight shift, lift, edging, etc., depends on the speed, the obliqueness of the traverse, the condition of the snow. In general, it can be said that the greater the speed, the sooner the synchronized movements of the turn begin. The start of the closing of the skis together is also a matter of speed. At good speeds, this closing is started with the lift and weight shift, so that the skis are parallel throughout most of the turn.

Figure 63—Basic Christiania from the Rear; Phases Identical with Those in Figure 62

107

In attempting light stem and body preparation, the skier has assumed the typical beginner's "boxing position" of the downhill arm. His stance is too erect, and his weight is on the uphill ski; in consequence, he will be unable to lift and swing into the turn. The phase of the turn corresponds to No. 2 of Figure 61.

Figure 64—Wrong Preparation for Basic Christiania

What Is Swing?

Earlier in this book, in discussing the fads of skiing and the fads in skiing nomenclature, we defended the use of the word "swing" by analogy with music. We reminded our readers that danceable music is swinging music, and that although jazz aficionados have switched their allegiance to cool and mannered jazz to which one listens rather than dances (or even taps the foot, heaven forbid!) there are still those who like to dance and for whom cool jazz and third-stream jazz are only part of the jazz scene, rather than all of it. We think of skiing as we do of dancing: both are rhythmical, fun, sociable, graceful, physically active (if you don't believe that, go to a discothèque and watch the kids dance), and for these reasons we're going to insist on using the word "swing" to characterize a family of turns which are fluid and fast, gracile and mellifluously exhilarating.

The christies are classed as swing turns, although the basic christie is a sort of mongrel, being started with vestiges of the slower speed turns, and then developing into a swing turn. Swing turns are those turns in which the position of the skis is virtually or entirely parallel throughout the turn, the turning being the result of speed plus shoulder, body, and knee action. The measured down-up-down of the lift and crouch, and the forceful use of circular motion and knee action, arm and hand motion, body banking—all these come under the heading of swing.

You may ask in what way counterswing and swing differ from countermotion and circular motion, as employed in the slower turns. In analysis, in a series of high-speed-camera "stopped" pictures, there would be no apparent difference. In actual execution, however, there is a great difference. You will recall that in the advanced snowplow turn we stemmed both skis, held the plow position for a while, made our countermotion, then went into the turn. In the stem turn, we stemmed the downhill ski and employed countermotion, then stemmed the uphill ski, then went into the turn. In a swing turn, the countermotion is not separated in time from the actual start of the turn. It is a springboard for the turn, not a distinct element which is a "held" position. In the basic christie, the counterswing is a preparation; the stemming of the downhill ski is also a "pushing off" onto the uphill ski; the countermotion is compressed in time, so that it is like a quick, short drawing back of the fist before a punch; and it is instantly followed by the punch itself, i.e., the swing.

The basic christie at good speed can be described then, as follows: traverse; preparation—flowing without break or pause into lift and swing; traverse again.

The foregoing words, or twice that number more expertly chosen, can't tell you as much about the basic christie as the pictures and diagrams can. Study both. The captions to the pictures explain salient points and describe what is happening. In the photographs, watch especially the position of knees, skis, edging and body. If any point seems unclear to you, reread the text, but the pictures tell the story best.

If you can do the basic christie when and as you want to, you are a skier. You may not be an expert, or a racer, or a ski acrobat, but you are out of the amateur ranks and a person to be looked upon with respect and admiration on any slope in the land.

Linking Basic Christianias

Now we are ready for a thrill: swinging downhill, in a series of linked basic christies, at good speed.

Linked christies are universally useful for descending a hill under control and for making you feel the master or mistress of the skier's world. Swinging down a hill in a series of long-radius christies used to be called *schwingen* in German (or, rather, Austrian, since skiing terms originated in that country) and it is still skiing de luxe in any language.

In the long-radius christies you use for linking, the counterswing for each link is made up mostly of body preparation and crouch (follow-through) from the previous turn, with very little stemming of the ski on the inside of the turn to come.

The individual christies which make up the links are not completed; that is, you start the next turn before the preceding one has brought you all the way around. There is no traverse between turns, either.

The action of shoulders, knees, and body is rhythmical and continuous; the "down" which is the end-phase crouch of one turn is also the "down" which is the starting phase of the next turn.

Just as one crouch serves as end phase of one turn and start of another simultaneously, so the final twist of body-and-shoulder action at the end of one turn serves as the preparation for the following turn.

Here are the actual steps in linking basic christianias:

You are in a traverse. Simultaneously stem lightly and prepare the body for circular motion. Immediately lift, weight-shift, and swing, all together. Follow through, so that as the turn comes around toward a new traverse, you are crouched and your body motion is at its fullest. Don't pause—you are wound up, set for the next turn in the opposite direction. Stem that downhill ski a little. Just enough so that you can use it as a springboard. Immediately push off from it into a new turn. Keep it up, turn after turn, in cadenced rhythm, right down the hill (Figures 65, 66 and 67).

Once again, it is the pictures, diagrams, and captions which will most reward careful study. Follow the sequences while going through

Figure 65—Linked Basic Christianias

Figure 66—Tracks of Linked
Basic Christianias

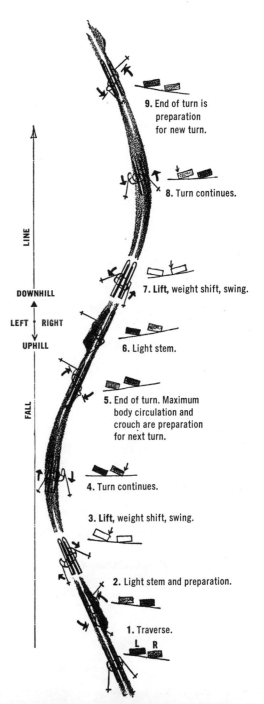

9. End of turn is preparation for new turn.

8. Turn continues.

7. Lift, weight shift, swing.

6. Light stem.

5. End of turn. Maximum body circulation and crouch are preparation for next turn.

4. Turn continues.

3. Lift, weight shift, swing.

2. Light stem and preparation.

1. Traverse.

LINE

DOWNHILL

LEFT | RIGHT

UPHILL

FALL

L   R

a dry run; that is, stand up and go through the movements, in so far as it is possible, while you scan the progressive stages of both pictures and diagrams. Note especially how and when the skis close, at what point the inside ski of a turn overtakes and leads the outside ski, how much and when the inside ski goes over onto its outside edge, and the depth of bend and position of the knees. Note the angle of the body, which leans in toward the center of the turn.*

* It sometimes happens that a christie, through faulty action in the early phases of the turn, does not "come around" as far as the skier desires. Usually, this is caused by improper timing, so that swing is used up before the turn is complete. There are two ways to rescue such a turn, neither desirable, to our way of thinking. One way is to shift the weight back: the weighting of the tails of the skis by leaning back makes them skid downhill. This will complete the turn (in the sense of getting the skis pointed in the desired direction) but it makes an abrupt and unattractive end phase and leaves the skier in an unstable position when he most needs stability. The forced skidding of the tails of the skis also retards speed and breaks rhythm. The other expedient (and one which is in vogue) is to employ extreme forward lean. The skier almost dives forward, hanging by the heels from his cables and leaning way out over the tips of his skis. The weighted tips act as an anchoring pivot point, and the unweighted rear parts of the skis slide freely over the snow, skidding in an arc of which the tips are the center. Here, again, the posture is potentially unstable; worse, if the snow is deep and soft, or if there is a thin crust, the ski tips, heavily weighted, may dive below the surface, throwing the skier forward and stopping him dead.

Once more, we reiterate our conviction that skiing on the whole of both skis, with the body weight centered, i.e., vertical to the skis and ready to adjust either forward or back, is the only safe and sure way to ski on every kind of snow, and under any circumstances. This vertical posture preserves speed, rhythm, and cadence. It helps the skier to carve clean turns, in which the skid is distributed over the curve instead of coming abruptly at the end. Most important, it is the position of greatest stability and latitude for adjusting to sudden changes.

Figure 67—Linked Basic Christianias

The Pole Christiania

While we yield to no one in our pleasure over the vastly increased popularity of skiing in the years since we first wrote a grammar of the art—which was the present volume's precursor—it does have its drawbacks. The population explosion has hit the ski slopes and, as a result, virginity—of snow, of course—has taken a bit of a licking. Smooth and unobstructed slopes, undulant and undefiled, are a rarity. At the more popular and populous resorts, rough terrain is a daily fact of ski life, what with man-made ruts, moguls, bare spots, sitzmarks and strayed gloves and headbands adding up to a virtual obstacle course. In such conditions, the use of a single pole as a pivot—in the pole christie—is an invaluable aid, contributing to the agility, versatility and security of the skier who must wend his way among man-made hazards and such natural impediments to ideal snow conditions as ice patches, rocks, stumps.

The pole christie used to be unpopular with purists: their principal objection to it was based on a feeling that the skier who learns it too early will overuse it—which is sometimes the case when the pole christie is taught before a sound basic christie without pole is learned. However, properly learned—and at the right time in one's progress—it is invaluable. And the right time is now, for it will not only improve your skiing at once, but will also prepare you for the extensive use of poles in today's advanced techniques.

In the pole christie, one pole is planted in the snow, ahead of the skier and toward the inside of the turn, and is used as a pivot point for the turn. This provides the skier with a security tripod consisting of two skis and one pole. The use of the pole also aids correct timing and helps precise carving of tight turns.

This is how the turn is performed. The skier is in a traverse and decides to turn. He prepares for the turn with countermotion and just as it is completed (that is, just before he lifts and swings) he plants the pole on the inside of the turn about two feet out to the side and about two thirds of the way from binding to ski tip. The instant the pole point enters the snow, he starts his turn, using the pole as a center.

The pole is used for stability and as a steadying agent. It also assures virtually automatic correct body preparation and thus preserves timing.

Practice linked, pole christies, all the way down a slope. As the swing of one turn comes to completion, the arm and hand on the outside of the turn are forward. That is the instant to plant that pole, so that the linked turn pivots around it.

Figure 68 shows the correct placing of the pole and Figure 69 shows linked pole christies.

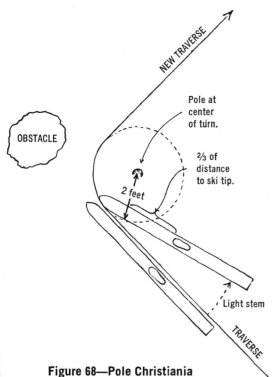

Figure 68—Pole Christiania

**Figure 69—Pole Christiania:
Close-up of Proper Placing of Pole
and Light Stemming**

**Figure 70—
Wrong Start of Pole Christiania**

The skier's position is not only wrong,
it is dangerous. Pole is too close to ski
tip, skier is bent over it, and pole
handle points at his body. In this position, if he were going fast, he could
injure himself badly.

113

Do's and Don'ts

Do launch your turn as soon as the lower ski is lightly stemmed.

Do enter your turn with good speed and keep your stem narrow.

Do let the arms and hands move around freely with the shoulders and use good knee action throughout the turn.

Do place your pole far enough to the inside of the turn (at least two feet) in executing the pole christiania.

Don't stem out with your uphill ski.

Don't try to make a slow-speed christie—please!

Don't shove the inside ski too far ahead when the skis close.

CHAPTER EIGHT

THE PURE OR STOP CHRISTIANIA

As a reward for your skiing efforts so far, we'll let you in on a secret about yourself. You have already executed a more advanced christie without knowing it. A parallel christie, at that—or anyway, a part of one.

Back a while, you were making a sliding stop from a traverse, as described under the section titled "Controlled Sideslipping." If you recall, you turned toward the slope from a traverse, with the skis parallel, by using good lift and circular motion. That maneuver was the infant pure christie, not yet grown up enough to be used from a schuss. Now we're ready to perfect the real thing.

The pure or stop christie is a stopping turn. It is an abrupt and rather spectacular swinging of the skis at right angles to the line of motion, followed immediately by a deep edging of both skis which brings you to a fast, skidding stop, usually accompanied by a flattering spume of snow and the ohs and ahs of the beginners. It is the only means of stopping quickly from a fast schuss.

The stop christie (a more descriptive and hence a better name than pure christie) takes courage to try, but it isn't hard to do and we'll work up to it gradually. The patience to practice it will be well rewarded, too, since between them the snowplow and the stop christies will remove the major mental hazard of the sport: fear of being unable to stop.

Let us begin with our stop from a traverse. Start again, as you did in controlled sideslipping, with a not too steep traverse and turn toward the slope, using good lift, plenty of countermotion, and lots of knee action as you come around.

Now try the same thing from a steeper, faster traverse. You'll have to express every motion with vigor, since you have farther to turn.

When you feel completely confident that you can stop from a quite steep traverse by turning toward the slope, you're ready to try the real stop christie. Let's start by coming down the hill in the fall line (schuss) and stopping when we come to the level runout.

Schuss down a practice slope, with good speed, and as you come out on the level, countermove your body to its fullest extent, then *lift*. At the instant when both skis (equally weighted and in schuss position) are almost pulled free of the snow, expend all your circular body

Figure 71—Stop Christiania from Schuss

1. Schuss position of skis; skier crouches in preparation for lift.
2. Lift and circular body motion.
3. As skis come across slope, skier is sinking into end phase of crouch.
4. Completion of circular motion and crouch, plus strong edging, bring the skier to a stop.

motion with rapidity and force. The skis will turn across the slope. Keep them very nearly flat as the weight comes down on them again, and, as you come downward in your crouch, edge them gradually on their uphill edges to stop your lateral skid.

The stop christie is quite a strain on the legs, and you must measure your capacity by edging quite slowly at first, and then speeding up the edging until you know what you can take. The more abrupt the turn, the more you will have to lean in toward its center to overcome centrifugal force, and the more of a strain the edging will be (Figures 71 and 72). However, a certain degree of quite automatic angulation will reduce the strain considerably.

Practice stop christies on the level runout before you attempt them in the middle of a hill. And then learn to do them on a hill, in the middle of the slope, near the top, near the bottom, wherever you want to. Now you have full control indeed. You can call yourself an accomplished skier—without stretching the truth.

Do's and Don'ts

Do look back to make sure no one is schussing down behind you before you make your stop.

Do keep your weight centered. Weight to the back will make the tails of the skis cross; weight too far forward will make the skis dive in deep snow and will make the tails skid too far around on packed snow.

Do use some angulation (pressing knees toward the slope), but also bank sharply with the entire body.

DON'T turn the skis with the feet. Use lift and vigorous circular motion.

DON'T try to make too tight a turn from high speed.

DON'T depend only on angulation at the end of the turn or the skis will run away from you in the direction they are edged; lean in with the entire body.

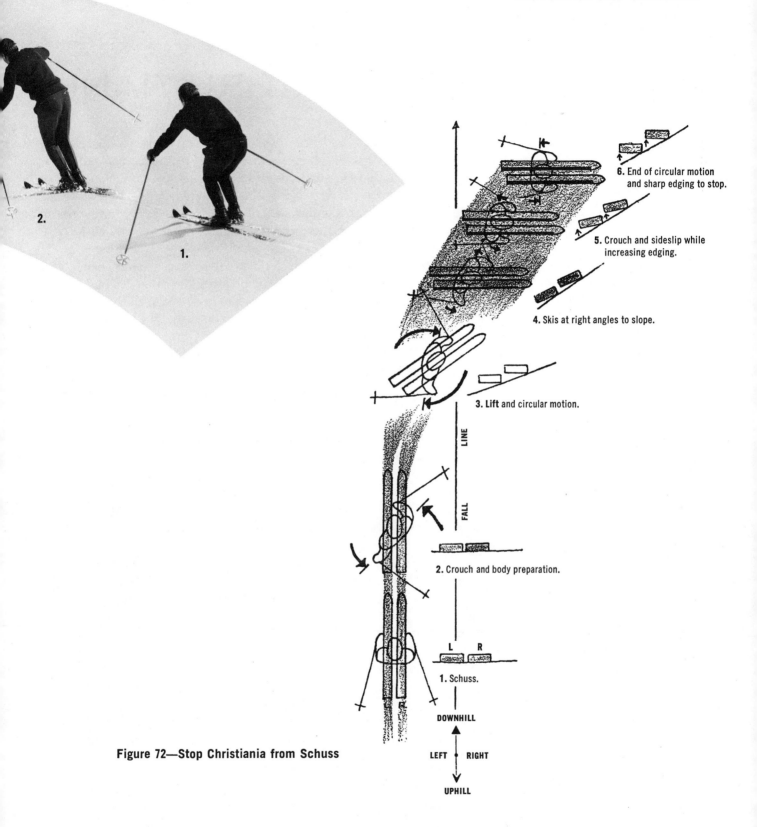

2.

1.

6. End of circular motion and sharp edging to stop.

5. Crouch and sideslip while increasing edging.

4. Skis at right angles to slope.

3. **Lift** and circular motion.

FALL LINE

2. Crouch and body preparation.

L   R

1. Schuss.

DOWNHILL

LEFT • RIGHT

UPHILL

Figure 72—Stop Christiania from Schuss

CHAPTER NINE

PARALLEL CHRISTIANIA

Up to this point—and we've come a long way—everything learned and everything explained has been a matter of technique and skill. The high-speed parallel christie is a matter of art and courage. You can ski well and happily all your life without ever executing one of these turns; their accomplishment will, however, give you a foretaste of heaven on earth, or, rather, heaven on skis, which the true enthusiast will tell you is still better.

Before going on to the turns, let us try to solve the controversy about whether or not all parallel turns are one and the same. To our minds, the term parallel christie applies to a family of turns, all those turns in which the skis are parallel throughout the turn. The purpose of the long-radius parallel turn is either to change direction or to maintain control—not to diminish speed. In a very limited sense speed *is* controlled; if a skier schussing a very steep slope feels he is gaining speed too fast, he can swing into a series of parallel turns to maintain a uniform speed with no acceleration. But the parallel turns are not used primarily for decreasing speed.

This family of turns must be performed on all the varied gradients, in all the varied snow conditions, with all the radii which the skier selects or encounters.

The parallel turns of long radius are the easiest to perform in the sense that they require least physical effort and involve fewest body motions. On the other hand, they are the hardest to learn, because they cannot be done by rote, or step by step, but are a matter of sensation. You have to have the feel of snow and skis and weight distribution; the turn, or curve, rather, is fluid and meltingly flowing; the movements involved are the same as those in the basic christie but most of them are reduced to muscular impulses rather than distinct movements, while some of them, like the preparatory countermotion, are so reduced and done so rapidly that they show up only in stop-action pictures of the turns. On the other hand, as these movements and swing become less pronounced, lift takes on added importance.

It would be foolish at this time to launch a long and detailed analysis of the parallel christies. If the reader does not by now know his skis well, and know how they respond to his body movements, no amount of reading will help. But for the man or woman who is confident and at home on skis, and who can do basic christies and stop christies easily and well, the following suggestions and explanations will prove helpful.

The turn is entered fast, usually from a traverse which is very near the fall line. Weight, of course, is equal on both skis, the axis of the skier's body being vertical with respect to the slope. There is diminished countermotion, and usually there is also an instantaneous and almost microscopic counterstemming of the inside ski of the turn as the skier gets set, although this is instinctive rather than intentional. Immediately, the skier lifts and starts circular motion and edging of the skis. (Actually, the lean of the body against centrifugal pull in the turn brings the skis up on their edges. It is as if the skier were a low-wing monoplane, his body the plane's body, his skis the plane's wings. As the plane banks a turn, the body of the plane tilts, but it does not bend, and the relationship of plane to wings stays the same—a right angle. So with the skier and his skis; he banks toward the center of the turn just enough to keep from skidding off sideways, and his skis stay in virtually the same relation to his body as they are when he is standing still on the level.) Relying on extreme angulation in these fluid parallel turns will lead to pressing in of the knees and possible catching of the uphill ski edge.

As the skier lifts, at the inception of the turn, his weight comes a little onto the outside ski, but the inside ski is not unweighted as much as in slower turns.

Some skiers describe their action at the start of a parallel turn in terms of very slight shifting of weight first from both skis to the inside ski of the turn, during the moment they are getting set, then from the inside ski to the outside ski. But even this weight shift is slight, and while the outside ski carries the larger part of the weight, the inside ski is by no means unweighted.

Similarly, the lift and crouch are neither so abrupt nor so obvious as in the basic christie, but they are extremely important, for it is the exact instant when the up changes to down (that is, the instant between the end of the up and the start of the down) that the skis are momentarily unweighted. The return of the weight to the skis must be protracted and attenuated by the crouching down again after the extension of the body in the lift. You've seen a baseball player soften the impact of a ball on his mitt by letting his hands come back toward his body as the ball is caught. You have seen a jumper use his bended

The skis bank the turn like the wings of a plane.

The body leans toward the center of the turn as if it were lying against the side of an imaginary cone.

knees to take up the shock of landing. Just so you must use your crouch to spread out the return of full weight to the skis over the entire length of the curve.

Edging in the parallel turns is an extremely delicate matter. On smoothly packed snow it is not crucial if a turn is spoiled by too much skid, or too abrupt ending due to too little or too much edging. But in deep snow or soft snow, and on rough terrain and among bumps and moguls, an error in edging can cause a spill at high speed. Edging in the parallel christie does not start the turn, though both skis are often fairly sharply edged at the completion. Here, again, the speed, the snow, the radius, are determining factors.

The following is an analysis of one parallel christie, to the left.

TRAVERSE: Skier is in an oblique traverse, close to the fall line, at good speed, moving from upper left of hill to lower right. Weight virtually equal on both skis, right ski very slightly in the lead, skis close together and parallel.

GET SET: Countermotion and crouch, both diminished, and of very short duration. Weight is solid, knees flexed and easy.

SWING: Immediately he is set, the skier starts lift and swing. Skis start to turn and weight comes over partially on the right ski. Body starts leaning in toward center of the turn, both skis are edged a little and equally. Knees are parallel, equally bent. Weight is centered—neither forward nor back. Left ski begins to move a very little ahead of right ski.

CROSSING FALL LINE: As the fall line is approached and crossed, the knees are flexing down, the swing is half expended, the edging of the skis, which remains equal, becomes a little more pronounced. Although the right ski remains somewhat more weighted than the left throughout the turn, the skier should attempt to ski on both skis as much as possible.

END OF TURN: Here the skier must preserve the smooth carving of the turn, neither skiing on the tips while he hangs from the cables, nor leaning back to weight the tails of the skis. Circular motion and knee bend are nearing their fullest expression. In another moment the skier will be ready to launch his next turn in the opposite direction, since completion of the turn leaves him set to start his parallel swing to the right.

That is a parallel christie analyzed, but you can't be expected to read as you ride your boards down a steep slope at speed, asking them to pause while you turn the page to find out what to do next. The analysis is designed to give you an understanding of what happens in the turn, and to provide a reference for the clearing up of difficulties encountered on the slope and confusions encountered in your mind as to just what happens when. One ingredient which is essential to high-speed parallel turns is courage. As a matter of fact, with courage and the confidence to maintain speed, the parallel christie is the easiest turn to execute on bad snow.

Here again you are urged to scan the pictures and diagrams of parallel christies (Figures 73 through 76) and the diagram of the

**Figure 73—Parallel Christiania
Going Away from Camera**

1. Skier is crouched and prepared.
2. Lift and circular motion begin.
3. Midturn and maximum lift.
4. Complete circular motion at end phase of turn. (From this position, skier can go into normal traverse stance or link a turn in the opposite direction.)

Figure 74—Linked Parallel Christianias

1. While schussing, skier starts sinking into crouch in anticipation of lift.
2. Full preparation for turn.
3. Lift and commence circular motion.
4. Midturn, full lift, continuation of circular motion.
5. Turn and full swing. (Note slight angulation.)
6. At end of turn, skier is fully prepared for turn in opposite direction.

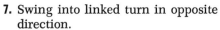

7. Swing into linked turn in opposite direction.
8. Skier is ready for another linked turn.

Figure 75—Track of Linked Parallel Christianias

dynamics of the swing turn (Figure 77), rather than depend on the text.

The aim of technique and form in every sport is the reduction of effort to a minimum, or, to put it positively, the maximum effectiveness of effort. These parallel turns, the ultimate in skiing, are also the ultimate in efficiency. And that efficiency can be learned only by

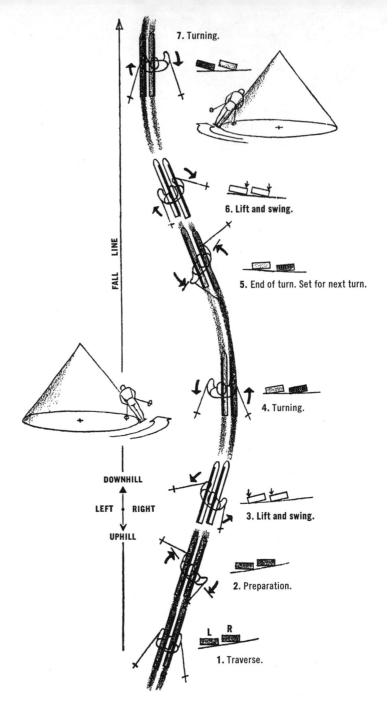

Figure 76—Parallel Christiania

practice. But an improper conception of the turn, a wrong notion of how it is done, can lead to your practicing it incorrectly, and you can learn bad habits as surely as you can good ones, if you persevere.

So study the text and the pictures and diagrams *with reference to your own performance.* Imitate consciously the attitudes of body, hands, poles, shoulders, ankles, and knees. You won't imitate them exactly no matter how hard you try. Each expert has his own unique

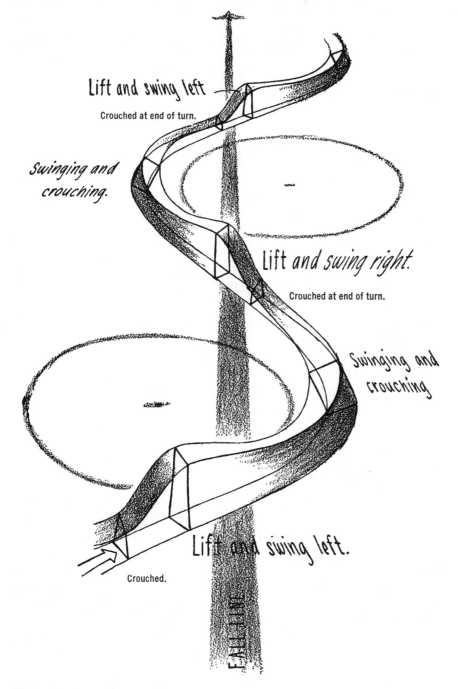

Lift and swing left

Crouched at end of turn.

Swinging and crouching.

Lift and swing right.

Crouched at end of turn.

Swinging and crouching

Lift and swing left.

Crouched.

Figure 77—Dynamics of the Swing Turn

style. But imitation is the easiest means of learning, and that's what you are after.

We hope you achieve it. If you do, you will know the sensations of the free-soaring bird, as you come swinging down a steep slope at high speed in linked parallel turns, sure of yourself, capable, controlled, alone with your skis and your skill and your strength pitted against a world of dazzling white, yet at the same time in tune with it.

CHAPTER TEN

ADVANCED TECHNIQUE

By now, presumably, the reader has mastered the basic maneuvers of open-slope skiing and has attained a good feeling for the sport in general. He is ready to consider those more advanced and specialized aspects of it which come under the general heading of advanced technique. These include the short swing and the much misunderstood wedeln. Before discussing and describing these adjuncts to good skiing, some observations are in order.

Unless you've been skiing alone in the wilderness, or on the mountains of the moon, you will have been exposed to at least one school of skiing which insists that it is *the* new religion of the slopes, that no other system of teaching skiing promises such wonders in such a short time, and that all previous methods of skiing and of instruction are obsolete. We applaud this enthusiasm for the new because anything which creates controversy, which suggests new ideas and new approaches, which gets people into excited discussions of skiing is, in general, good for the sport. We also know that, historically, these extreme attitudes and outlandish techniques gradually simmer down or vanish, depending on how much that is useful can be distilled from them. The whole progress of skiing can be seen as experimentation, extreme departures, and then the gradual gleaning of a few grains of good skiing sense to add to the whole of skiing lore and the art of the sport.

So, though we have no quarrel with any of the multitudinous schools of teaching and of skiing, we would like to warn you here that much that is being offered as new is the rediscovery of techniques which have already been discarded as not only not new but not suitable. We would like to warn you that in skiing, as in any other sport, the extreme and the bizarre may look interesting, but they have no place in teaching or in the development of controlled skiing with technique suitable to all ski conditions. Finally, we would like to re-emphasize our belief that a system of teaching—whether that expounded in this book or any other—can be good and correct only if everything learned from the very first day is used, if everything learned progresses normally and logically from what went immediately before to what immediately follows, and if the ultimate aim is mastery.

It is interesting to note in the development of various schools and styles of skiing that, however different they may be, they have certain things in common. Usually they originate with one man who himself is a great skier but who also happens to be something of an individualist. Frequently this is connected with his physique; a man who is short in stature, extremely strong in the legs, and rather heavy may become a championship skier by developing a style of his own designed to take advantage of his particular physical configuration and to overcome whatever drawbacks it may present. Should such a man be a consistent race winner, it is a very good bet that by the next season there will be thousands of eager-beaver skiers striving to imitate him, however unsuitable his technique may be for them. By the same token, it is quite possible that this individualistic skier will become an honest and dedicated believer in his system for everybody.

Those who have any memory in the art at all will recall the heyday of Dick Durrance, the great skier and inventor of the so-called dipsy-doodle—which thousands of skiers tried to emulate and very few achieved. Those with a memory will recall the excitement with which the extreme ruade (*ruade*—literally, "cow-kick," that is, a sharp kicking up of the heels accompanied by a forward diving of the body), as employed by Emile Allais, swept skiing by storm. They will remember the days when the word on everybody's tongue was "parallel"—"Learn parallel from the start," "Ski parallel!" There was a period when the word "vorlage" was interpreted so radically that thousands of skiers hung over the tips of their skis by their heel cables even when going down a very gentle slope. Turning under these circumstances was incredibly difficult; a snowplow with no weight on the heels didn't plow. But vorlage was the word, and that's the way everybody tried to ski, despite the ensuing proliferation of "nose christies."

By now it should be clear that skiing, like every other sport, and every other human activity for that matter, entails fads and fancies as well as solid procedures. Far be it from us to say that the technique of the sport has never changed and will never change. That would be foolish. We are not prophets and we know that there have been changes, some of them dictated by changes in terrain, others by changes in what people want out of skiing, others by developments in equipment. Certainly the future will see further changes. All we say, and we repeat it over and over again in this book, is that we believe that by following the orderly procedure outlined in these pages and by attempting to ski in the manner described, the novice, the intermediate and the expert will be skiing with more pleasure, more precision, more style, more flair and more control than can be achieved by any other method of which we know.

Skiing Over Bumps

The great traffic on today's most popular runs and slopes has created a condition rarely encountered years ago. This is the well-traveled slope which is studded with man-made bumps, or, as they are called, moguls. These are not to be confused with the long, natural ridges and undulations generally encountered on most virgin slopes. Moguls tend to be steeper, smaller and somewhat convex in shape—almost conical. They occur fairly close together and there are regular grooves and valleys between them. To the practiced skier they provide challenge, variety and fun. To the person who does not know how to cope with them, they present a formidably forbidding problem. We shall now attempt to solve that problem for these people.

It is virtually impossible to ski bumpy or moguled terrain using the snowplow turn or the stem turn, as the grooves and valleys between moguls are so narrow as to make it impossible to let the skis assume the plow position. Since moguls develop on the steeper slopes, however, and are not likely to occur on nursery and lower-intermediate slopes, it is unlikely that the recreational skier will encounter them before he has fully mastered the basic christie. Accordingly, we will now discuss and explain how to negotiate moguls applying the basic christie. (In the event that a stem-turn skier does encounter a bumpy snow field, the best procedure for him to follow in negotiating it is via long, shallow traverses with good traverse position and elasticity in the knees to absorb the oncoming bumps—see Figure 30. If it is necessary to turn before coming to a smoother part of the slope where the stem turn is possible, he should attempt to sideslip to a stop from the top of a bump and then make a kick turn to traverse in the opposite direction.)

Basic Christiania Over Bumps

The major difference in the basic christiania as described earlier in this book, and that which is used in skiing over and among moguls, is the use of the poles and the shortness of the turn. If you will go back to the description of the pole christiania (page 110) you will see how the pole is used to make a tighter turn to avoid an obstacle. In employing the basic christie over bumps, the poles are held farther forward than in normal skiing position, the hands are higher, and in this way either pole may be quickly placed in the snow to initiate a turn. As usual, in descending a slope with christianias linked by traverses, the skier in the traverse position has good elasticity, looks ahead, and tries to estimate where his turn will be made. In skiing among moguls, the place you will pick is the top of one of these bumps, which will give you, in addition to your usual body lift, the lift provided by the shape of the bump. With this additional lift, and with the pole employed as in the pole christie, you will be able to execute a much sharper turn than the normal basic christiania and will be in the new traverse before entering the next groove. This is the full purpose of this maneuver, i.e., to make use of the lift provided by the bump and to complete the turn before the skis are in the hollow of the next groove. Obviously, this necessitates much faster action throughout the turn and hence much more accurate timing. (See Figures 78, 79, 80, 81.)

The procedure may be described as follows: In his traverse the skier skis as squarely on both skis as possible, uphill ski leading to feel the way, knees very elastic and responsive to variations in the slope, poles held somewhat forward in readiness for use, arms away from the body sufficiently to give balancing action, skier looking ahead to plan his turn. His knees may be likened to shock absorbers, his poles act like the stabilizers on a plane's wings. Should he gain too much speed, he sideslips a little at the tops of moguls (the only part of the terrain where there is an opportunity to do this, since it is impossible in the grooves where speed rapidly accelerates) and so is ready when he comes to the turning place, with the correct speed and the correct stance to execute his turn.

Suppose this is to be a right turn. Simultaneously the skier makes a short stem with the right ski and plants the right pole about as far forward as the point where the shovel (i.e., the curved and wider portion of the front of the ski) of the ski first makes contact with the snow and about a foot out to the side. (The distance from the skier and from the ski at which the pole is placed will obviously vary with the speed, the terrain and the size of the skier; the figure given here is average.) The instant the stem is made and the pole is placed, the skier swings and closes the skis vigorously, with forceful circular motion, so that by the time he is in the next groove and picking up speed he is once more squarely over his skis and *with* them. By the time the skier is through the groove and at the top of the next mogul, he is thus already prepared for the left turn. Now the left pole is placed and the left ski stemmed, the skier swings and he's in the next groove. Thus, with correct pole placement, correct stemming, and correct circular motion, the skier is constantly in control of his skis, above them, and always ready after each turn and short traverse for the next turn in the opposite direction.

It is important here to consider the critical nature of timing in this maneuver. Obviously, if the turn is executed too slowly it will not be completed in time to have the skis parallel going into the groove. And even if it is so completed, there is the possibility that the outside shoulder will not come around fast enough to put the skier squarely over his skis as the turn completes (see later discussion of delayed shoulder action, intentional and unintentional). This delay results in the skis running ahead of the body—as we already know, a very unstable state of affairs which leads to the "sitz christie." There is an equal and opposite failure in timing which is excessive circular motion. In his anxiety to be there on time and to be sufficiently expressive in

Figure 78—Basic Christiania Over Rough Terrain and Bumps— from Schuss (*as seen from the front*)

1. Schuss. Skier has selected the place for his turn.
2. Slight crouch, light stem, pole coming into position to act as pivot for the turn.
3. Pole is in position, skier lifts and initiates circular motion.
4. Midturn in the groove. (Note slight normal angulation.)
5. End phase of turn with skier in proper position for initiating next turn in opposite direction.

Figure 79—Basic Christiania Over Rough Terrain and Bumps
(*as seen from the outside of the turn*)

1. Traverse.
2. Light stem, pole placement, and preparation.
3. Rapid, confined lift and circular motion begin.
4. Midturn.
5. Skier is banking his turn for proper edging and in order to keep entire body perpendicular to skis and shoulders squared over them.
6. The turn is being carved with the skier in full control and body position relaxed and flexible.
7. End phase of turn. Note full body circular motion; the skier is fully prepared for turn in opposite direction.

his swing, the skier overdoes it, with the result that the ski tips run into the side wall of the bump immediately following the one on which the turn was initiated and catch there—dumping the skier. Both errors of timing—that is, the delayed shoulder and excessive circular motion—tend to place the skier's weight on the uphill ski, which is unstable and hence incorrect.

1. As bump is approached, skier is already in prepared position for circular motion and pole planting.
2. At the moment of pole planting, skier is slightly crouched and lightly stemming.
3. Lift and circular motion.
4. End phase of turn and ready for next turn in opposite direction.

Figure 80—Basic Christiania Over Rough Terrain and Bumps (*as seen from inside of turn*)

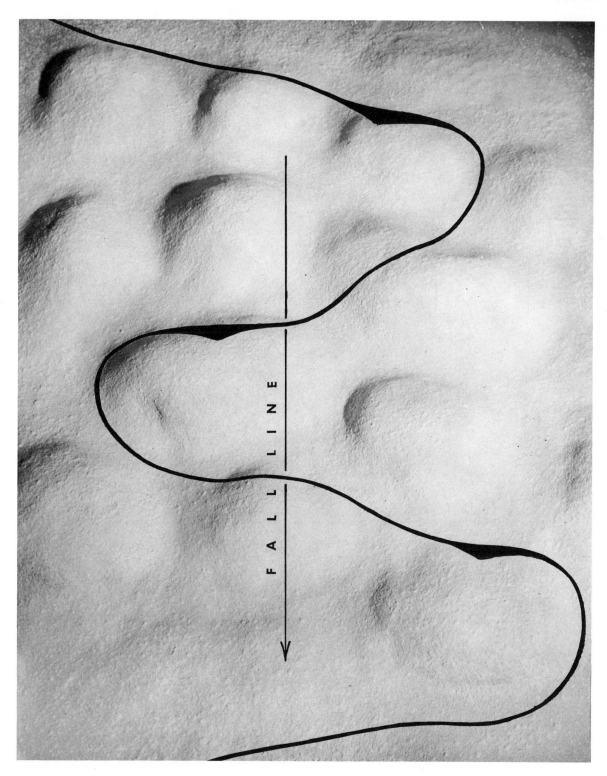

FALL LINE

Figure 81—Basic Christiania Over Rough Terrain and Bumps

The Critical Importance of Preplanning

Bearing in mind the foregoing, let's ski a slope which is full of bumps and see how we work.

Before starting out we scan the slope to try to predetermine our course down it. This pausing to estimate the situation is the mark of the intelligent skier, be he beginner or expert. Many skiers—even some seasoned experts—in their anxiety to get started, launch themselves down the slope and are immediately in trouble because they don't know where to go and there isn't time to figure it out en route. By the same token, once the tentative line is chosen the good skier will be constantly looking ahead to continue the job of estimating what lies before him. It is a good idea, before starting out, to plan the first three or four turns—that is, where they will be made and at about what speed. With this plan in mind, it is easy enough while executing the first three or four turns to look ahead and plan the next few. The aim of this preplanning is to assure control and rhythm—the latter an absolute essential in skiing over bumps, where timing is of the essence. In this connection, it is not timidity but only good sense to choose not the worst and most difficult and rugged bumps, but those which provide the easiest turning. It will usually be rugged enough!

Once you start out, the traverse position is again sound and squarely with the skis, the uphill ski leading and the knees whippy and elastic. Poles are gripped firmly and are held at the ready for placing in the turns. Some people, in attempting to use the poles in bumpy terrain, tend to swing them from the wrist like pendulums. Obviously, when one is reaching ahead to plant a pole it will be swung forward a certain amount, just as it will be swung back a certain amount when it leaves the snow at the end of the turn. However, this pendulum motion should be kept to a reasonable minimum, since what is desired is stability and precision and these can be attained only with a firm wrist and a firm grip on the pole. Furthermore, the natural and correct action of the upper body is encouraged by the arcing reach of the entire arm, from shoulder to hand, rather than by keeping arms and shoulders rigid and swinging the pole from the wrist.

You are now approaching the bump where you have planned your first turn. As you get to its top, you simultaneously stem and plant your pole, swing with good circular motion, close skis, and you're in your new traverse. You will notice that we did not mention lift. Of course you will lift; you have been having lift dinned into your ears since the very early parts of this book. But because of the lifting action provided by the terrain, your lift will be comparatively confined. In fact, by now it should be a natural and automatic part of your skiing rather than a thing you consciously strive for in taking off from the top of a mogul.

If you have executed this first turn correctly, you will shoot out of the groove following the turn in perfect position for your next turn in the opposite direction. Out of the groove, up the mogul, stem and pole plant, confined (that is, moderate) lift, swing, and you're back in the next groove ready for your next turn in the other direction.

Properly executed, this sort of descent will not only be effectively handled by you but will give you a delicious sense of floating—almost of flying—when you initiate your turns; but this delightful sensation must be bought with correct timing, fast action, springy knees, quick—almost kicky—lift, and correct weight shift from ski to ski during the tight christie turns. There is one other important way in which this basic christie differs from the earlier open-slope basic christie and the earlier-described pole christie. In the christiania under discussion over bumps and moguls, the pole is actually used not only as a timing device but also, as needed, for additional support.

Since it is not too likely that you will have success in your first attempts, it may be valuable to list here the eleven most frequent causes of failure and their cures.

1. Many skiers are so pleased at having executed the first turn that they fail to follow through rapidly enough to be in position for the next turn when it is time to execute it.
2. Many skiers who have been cautioned against trying to use the pole as a brake in their earlier efforts are now afraid to make adequate use of it as a stabilizer in turning over moguls.
3. Although you can control your speed by quick, short sideslips in the traverses, once you are in a groove don't try to check your speed or your ski tips will catch on the side walls of the surrounding bumps. Similarly, if in turning into a groove you try to shorten the radius of the turn in order to check your speed, you will find yourself using too much circular motion and again the ski tips will catch. Once in the groove, don't fight it—ride it, glide it.
4. Be sure to confine your lift so as not to extend your knees too far. You need them flexed for the fast action which immediately follows the lift. Let the mogul do most of the work for you.
5. Hold your poles firmly and reach with the arms, not by using the pole pendulum fashion.
6. Start your christies over bumps from a fairly shallow traverse. Don't attempt to follow the fall line.
7. Don't let the inside ski of the turn move ahead more than three to four inches, as this might cause it to catch the side wall of the bump you are turning away from. Advancing the ski farther than this will also render it virtually weightless, so that if it does catch on a small unevenness, the skis may scissor open disastrously.
8. In attempting to control speed in the groove, some skiers try to ski on the uphill wall of the groove instead of on its floor. Hugging

the side wall of a bump is a sure way to have the skis slip out from under you. Stay in the groove and if your skiing position is correct the acceleration will be exhilarating instead of frightening.

9. Never attempt to stem in the groove. Wait until the groove opens up.

10. Don't exhaust your knee action too soon in the turn; gradually sink from your lift position as the turn progresses, so that you finish your forward circular motion in the groove and are ready for the next lift at the top of the next mogul.

11. If you're going too fast for comfort and there is not enough space between grooves for a sideslip check during the traverse, look ahead for alternative routes over and around moguls to make your descent shallower and farther from the fall line.

Parallel Turns on Bumpy Terrain

The skier who has mastered the parallel turn should find it a great joy to ski moguls employing this turn. Very briefly, what the parallel skier does is to use the walls of the moguls just as a racing driver uses a banked turn on a speedway. Thus, each bump or mogul will help tremendously in initiating and completing the parallel turn. The two major ways in which the parallel descent of bumpy terrain and the basic-christie descent differ are: (1) The parallel skier skis somewhat closer to the fall line; (2) since the skier's speed is greater, he initiates his turns *before* reaching the tops of the moguls. In general, the parallel turn as employed over bumps differs from the basic christiania as employed over bumps just as the two turns differ on smooth terrain. That is, the use of the pole for timing and stability, and as the center of the radius of the turn, comes into play in the parallel turn for bumpy terrain just as it does in the basic christiania for bumpy terrain. Similarly, too—to an even greater degree—the lift is quite confined, since the combination of speed and moguls does the lifting for you almost entirely. Should you use exaggerated lift at good speed in such terrain, you'd find yourself flying through the air instead of executing a turn.

Figures 82, 83, and 84 show parallel turns made on steep slopes with rough snow and among moguls. Figure 85 shows the use of the hook (explained on page 138) as a speed regulator. Figure 86 shows the double-pole parallel turn, in which both poles are used simultaneously, for even greater stability, when extremely rough conditions are encountered at speed. Its execution is much the same as the single-pole parallel turn; note (in Figure 86) that shoulder action is not inhibited by use of both poles. Figure 87 shows the course of the parallel skier down a slope studded with moguls.

Figure 82—Parallel Turn on Bumpy Terrain from Traverse

1. Skier is emerging from turn and going into traverse.
2. Traverse. Skier is prepared for parallel turn. NOTE: Arm and hand are in position for planting of pole.
3. Pole is planted, lift and circular motion have started.
4. Midphase of turn.
5. In the groove and in full control.
6. End phase of turn with skier in complete readiness for pole planting and body motion for turn in opposite direction.

Figure 83—Parallel Turn on Bumpy Terrain from Traverse
(*going away from camera*)

1. Body is prepared for turn and pole is in position for planting.
2. Pole is planted, lift and circular motion have begun. NOTE: You can see the shadow of the heels of the skis showing effect of strong lift.
3. Carving the turn into the groove.
4. In the groove. Note that continuing circular motion is keeping the shoulders at right angles to the ski and body is banking the turn.
5. End of the turn. Skier is completely prepared for turn in opposite direction.

Figure 84—Employing the Hook to Parallel Turn on Bumpy Terrain and Very Rough Snow

1. In traverse, the skier is in position for planting pole and hooking to establish his platform for the turn that follows.
2. The hook. Pole was planted near tips, skier has already advanced so that pole, in full use, is almost at mid-ski.
3. Lift and forward circular motion; the forward circular motion has naturally and automatically lifted the heels of the skis from the snow.
4. Carving the turn; shoulders square over skis.
5. Coming out of the turn in full control.
6. Turn is completed with maximum circular motion and skier is in position for turn in opposite direction.

Now let's consider an actual beginning of a bumpy-slope descent for the parallel skier. First—and again we are consciously repeating ourselves in the hope of driving home this important lesson—look ahead and plan ahead before taking off. The course you choose is a little closer to the fall line than with the basic christiania. Approaching the first bump with flexible and elastic knee action, shoulders square above the skis, arms held somewhat away from the body for balance, and poles at a slight angle and firmly gripped, and with the uphill ski leading by about three inches, the parallel swing with confined lift is started as you approach the top of a bump. This confined lift, though slight, is not dragged out but is short and dynamic, a definitive and rapid movement. Circular motion, too, will be minimized. The weight distribution is about 60 per cent—40 per cent, that is, with 60 per cent on the outside ski.

You will recall that in the basic christie the turn was completed before entering the groove and the skier went down the center of the groove. In the parallel turn, the end phase of the turn is completed in the groove with the skier perhaps one-third up the downhill wall of the groove in the typical banked parallel position—only now the banking is the result of the shape of the groove rather than the edging of the skis. When the skier comes out of the groove, he will be ready for his next swing in the opposite direction. In this turn the danger of excessive circular motion is greater, since everything must be done more quickly and too much circular motion in the end phase will not find the outside pole ready for the next turn in the opposite direction. If you are late with the outside hand reaching with its pole for the next bump, your body will be behind your skis and you will not be in a position to make the next turn safely. The correct parallel turn on bumpy terrain demands that the short, confined lift be made with both legs and both knees—which will insure keeping the skis parallel. Once this timing is properly mastered the turn is deliciously easy, since it is the centrifugal force of the skier which permits him to use the wall of the groove to bank his turn effortlessly. In fact, this centrifugal principle makes it possible to ski parallel without skiing tremendously fast. Given good balance, good timing, and a little practice, it is the easiest parallel skiing there is.

The Hook

Now comes a very important refinement in the parallel skiing of bumpy terrain—one which we have never seen explained anywhere else. We have chosen to call it the hook. The hook is used to control the speed in the parallel descent of bumpy terrain. Here's how it works: Just before the lift, the skier performs a very short and energetic parallel sideslip which almost instantly is terminated with sharp edge bite achieved with angulation. This is the hook and it has several advantages in addition to checking the speed. In the first place, it provides the skis with a firm take-off platform which makes the short, kicky lift more secure and easier. In the second place, if the skier is employing the elastic rhythm that he should, the hook will provide not only a platform but an actual springboard which in effect launches him into his turn. As we said, this sideslip is short and abrupt, with the use of angulation for sharp, firm, instant biting of the edges at the end of the short skid, immediately followed by the springboard thrust from the launching platform the hook provides.

There is another alternative open to any skier who wishes to avail himself of it. This is to forget the hook, to prolong and exaggerate the lift, and to plant the pole tip so far back that the skier's body will fall well behind the skis in timing. This maneuver is employed when the skier desires to leave the terrain and sail into the woods. We assume no responsibility for the resulting damage to the local forestation.

Figure 85—Detail View of the Hook
(*as seen from the rear*)

1. Natural traverse position.
2. The hook, showing sharp edging and natural angulation. The skier is ready to plant his pole.
3. Lift and forward circular motion; the forcefulness of this maneuver naturally lifts the heels of the skis momentarily, thus facilitating turning.

141

Figure 86—Double-Pole Parallel Turn on Bumpy Terrain

1. Skier is crouched and both poles have been planted.
2. Lift and forward circular motion.
3. End phase of turn.

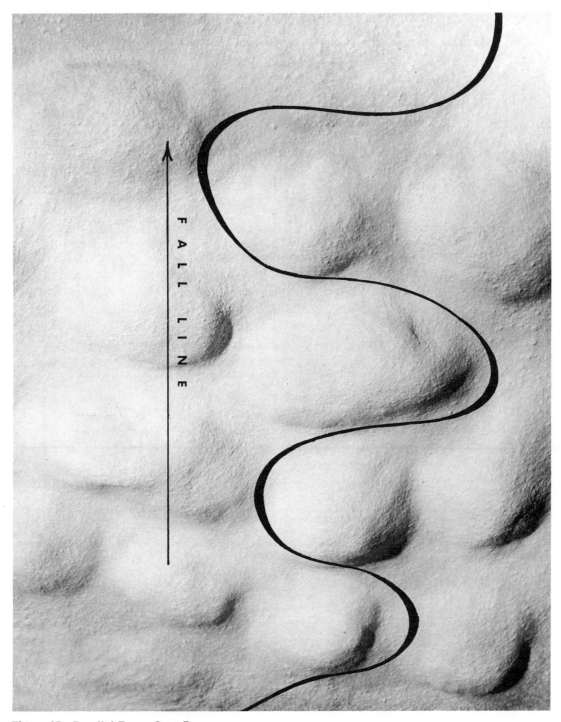

FALL LINE

Figure 87—Parallel Turns Over Bumps

Airplane Turn

This turn is extremely useful for skiing bumpy terrain studded with moguls, but it is not essential to the recreational skier's repertory. However, it is highly recommended. It may seem to the beginner or the intermediate skier that his greatest joy would be to descend a slope day after day in perfect, linked parallel turns. He would not believe it, but it is true that once he has achieved this so-much-desired goal he may find himself wishing for some variety. This the airplane turn will provide. Thus it has the double virtue of being extremely useful on bumpy terrain and of giving the skier something a little different and a little more spectacular to do.

A fair degree of expertness is required for the correct execution of the airplane turn. Once this is attained, however, the turn itself is not difficult. Generally, it originates out of a fast traverse. The skier literally takes off from the top of a mogul, executes his parallel turn while in the air and lands in the groove, lined up for the finish of his turn. The airplane turn is extremely useful for clearing several close-together, very sharp bumps at once. Thus employed, the turn requires the kind of judgment of speed and distance that only experience can give you. However, this experience can be readily acquired by learning the turn over a single bump. (See Figures 88, 89, and 90.)

Let's go through the motions of one such airplane turn. Let's assume you've chosen the bump from which you will take off and you are approaching it in good traverse position, at considerable speed, looking well ahead, weight nicely distributed on both skis, knees elastic. From the normal crouch position as you come up the bump, you prepare to plant your pole at the very top of the bump, where you will lift up strongly and with full extension of the legs (remember, you want to fly!), and the combination of the terrain and the vigorous lift sends you into the air.

Once you are airborne (but not waiting; this is all one continuous motion), your outside hand and arm come around exactly as in the parallel turns on the ground, an arcing motion accompanying the turning of the skis, which is accomplished in the air. While executing the turn you will also be drawing up your knees so that the parallel skis are close to the body and as far from the surface of the snow as you can get them. Below you now is the top of the bump you are jumping over; the drawing up of the feet close to the body is important to make sure that you clear this crest, since it is your purpose to land in the groove on the other side of it. Now you prepare for the landing, which will not be difficult if your body has turned to the correct angle for skiing in the landing groove. But before you land, you straighten your legs somewhat (although you must not straighten them all the way and lock the knees, which would make your landing an upsetting jolt). Your purpose is to extend your legs so that as the skis come down onto the snow you will have ample reserve spring in your knees and

Figure 88—Airplane Turn

1. Approaching take-off at crest of mogul.
2. Maximum crouch to initiate flight.
3. Take-off. Strong lift, vigorous forward body motion and pole used as pivot all serve to initiate the mid-air turn.
4. In the air and turning.
5. Midphase of turn.
6. Skier's body fully extended in preparation for absorbing shock of landing.
7. As the skier lands, entire body flexes from the previously extended position, so that landing is smooth and shock is completely absorbed.
8. End phase of turn with skis parallel in new direction.

legs to absorb the shock. Just as a ballplayer in catching a fast ball lets the glove come back to stop the motion of the ball gradually, so you let your knees flex so that you settle onto the snow instead of pounding down onto it. If the knees are locked, you can't do this. Similarly, if the knees are still tucked up when you land you won't have any elasticity to absorb the shock. As we said, judgment is required—and fine timing—in estimating the distance to be traveled and the speed required, and, very importantly, in making sure that the skis are lined up with the groove in which one is going to land. But once these niceties are mastered, the airplane turn is one of the most delightful in the advanced skier's repertory, since it gives him the ultimate sensation of floating.

1. Approaching crest from which turn will be launched.
2. Skier is in crouched launching or springboard position and ready to plant pole.
3. At the moment of jump-off.
4. Turning in air so that landing will be in the groove.
5. Landing with parallel skis lined up in the groove.
6. End phase of turn.

Figure 89—Low Airplane Turn on Extremely Rough and Bumpy Terrain with Short, Choppy Moguls

Jumping and Prejumping

There is one other maneuver in high-speed skiing over bumps, especially when the slope is steep, in which the skier voluntarily leaves the ground to fly through the air. This is the jump. It is used for two purposes: (1) to pass over one or more in a series of close-together, sharp-sloped bumps, by jumping over them; (2) to safely negotiate a very steep drop-off. The jump itself is made as in the airplane turn—only without turning. As in the airplane turn, the skis are drawn up to the body during flight and the legs are then extended to act as shock absorbers in landing.

The critical action is the timing of the take-off. If one does not prejump a sharp drop-off, the flight path extends to its leveler runout—with a resultant shock in landing—and the time in flight is protracted to the point where the skier's control may be drastically

Figure 90—Airplane Turn Over a Bump
(*Dotted line shows actual flight.*)

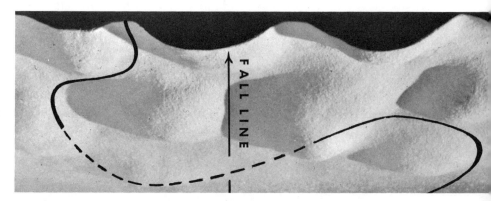

FALL LINE

diminished. If, in jumping over close-set bumps, the jump is made too late, the impetus provided by the take-off bump will be lacking and the flight will be too low and too short. Figure 91 shows the correct take-off locations for these jumps.

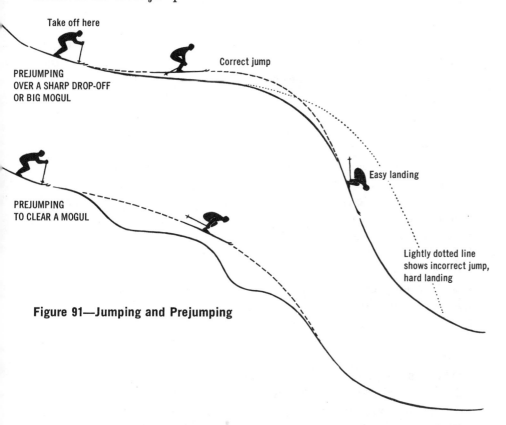

Take off here

Correct jump

PREJUMPING
OVER A SHARP DROP-OFF
OR BIG MOGUL

Easy landing

PREJUMPING
TO CLEAR A MOGUL

Lightly dotted line
shows incorrect jump,
hard landing

Figure 91—Jumping and Prejumping

Moguls and Form

Throughout this book, we have stressed the importance and the virtues of executing ski maneuvers with good form. However, it is a sad fact that many skiers so overdo attention to grace and beauty in their skiing that they become prima donnas of the slope and sacrifice fun, speed, and capacity to handle a variety of terrain in the interest of always seeming to look perfection itself. The fact is that on steep and bumpy and rough terrain, even the world's greatest skiers will find themselves momentarily in somewhat less than perfect postures. This is only normal; the rapid adjustments of every part of the body in maintaining equilibrium at high speed over bumpy terrain will inevitably produce some awkward postures. Undesirable as these may seem, they're far superior to falling down with a thud with the skis perfectly parallel and the arms exactly as they are pictured in the travel brochure. Alternatively, there are skiers who might be likened to hot-rodders whose sole aim is to come careening down the fall line willy-nilly at what is too often literally breakneck speed. You, the good and sensible skier who skis for fun and not merely to impress the onlookers or to break records, will choose the sensible middle course.

CHAPTER ELEVEN

WEDELN

Wedeln has become a magic word in skiing. Everybody talks about it, some people know what it is, some people know how to do it, some people do it for fun, some people do it all wrong without realizing it. There are actually excellent uses for this maneuver.

The term itself, translated into English, is extremely descriptive. Wedeln might be roughly translated as tail-wagging; the maneuver on skis consists of wagging the tails of the skis from side to side in short arcs while the tips continue in the direction of forward motion. The function of wedeln is fourfold. First, it is employed in taking the shortest (closest to the fall line) route down a bumpy, mogul-studded run. A wedeln skier's course down a mountain approximates the path that would be taken by a liquid poured from the top. (See Figure 104.) Second, it is employed to control speed in descending corridors and narrow trails, where it performs the same function at high speed that the snowplow does at low speed; i.e., it gives the skier control and the means for retarding his speed where there is no room for downhill traverses. Third, wedeln is employed in slalom. Fourth, it is a happy, dancing sort of way to have free-wheeling fun, not at all unlike the twist.

There is one extremely unfortunate drawback to wedeln—and you will be pleased to learn that it is completely unnecessary. We refer to the fact that today far too many skiers learn wedeln and use it to the exclusion of all other ski maneuvers—they wedel the day away instead of having a complete repertory of skiing technique (including wedeln) with which to fully enjoy the skier's art and with which to take advantage of (rather than to suffer from) variations in slope, terrain, snow conditions, and the desire to have fun on the mountain. By our standards, that kind of fun entails using the whole mountain as one uses the whole range of his skills—as opposed to spending the day at one specific ski run, riding up the lift and wedeling down, which to us seems to be about as much fun as running on a treadmill or doing one cha-cha step all night long.

In the ensuing pages we will be describing four specific kinds of wedeln: the basic, or recreational wedeln; the wedeln suitable to negotiating rough terrain; the snake, or serpentine wedeln; and the employment of wedeln for short, sharp swings. There is a fifth sort of wedeln which we call the mambo wedeln; this—like the Reuel swing or turn—is more of a for-fun-and-show-off maneuver than a useful one; it will be described and explained after we learn the useful wedeln maneuvers.

Before attempting to learn wedeln, something of its dynamics must be understood. The side-to-side fanning of the skis is accomplished with lift. The distance of the side-to-side travel of the tails of the skis is short, the motion is rapid, and at the end of each "wag" the skis are strongly edged so that they bite in (with strong yet automatic angulation) and instantaneously provide a push-off platform for the wag in the opposite direction. Thus, with quick lifts between wags, the ski tails are wagged back and forth rhythmically from platform to platform, with no pause in between. This tail-wagging with lift is accompanied by use of the poles, much the same as in the basic christie and the parallel turn over bumps. You may have heard—and it may be—that one need not be a very advanced skier to learn proper use or execution of wedeln. We beg to differ with this opinion. It is our belief that the true and correct wedeln is best learned after one has attained sufficient skill to bring to it the necessary rapid and exact timing and knowledge of edge control which it requires.

Pre-wedeln Exercises

There is one way to initiate yourself into the mysteries of wedeln which is physically rather exacting but may well pay off in quickly earned dividends. You might wish to try it. If so, pick a gentle slope which is smooth and hard-packed. Hold yourself in the fall line with skis parallel by planting both poles to the sides of the ski tips at about the point where the shovel touches the surface. Gripping the poles firmly and letting the pole straps support a good part of your weight, try wedeln in place. Maintaining the position you are in with the poles, you fan the tail ends of the skis from side to side. Do it this way: Literally hop and arc the back ends of the skis to the right, edge sharply, immediately take off from the platform thus provided with a heel-thrusting hop, and wag the tails of the skis to the opposite end of the arc. Don't pause there, but again hop, heel thrust, edge; hop, heel thrust, edge; hop, heel thrust, edge—until you get the rhythmic feeling of wedeln. (When you wedel at speed on a slope you will be lifting and fanning the heels of the skis, rather than hopping and arcing them.) The tails of the skis lightly stroke the snow; they are not lifted clear of it. This is more difficult to accomplish in the standstill position than in motion, but it should be borne in mind and striven for just the same. In motion, the stroking (as opposed to jumping) is natural and much easier. You will notice that the pressure on the poles alternates just as the edging of the skis alternates. When you take off from the left wag toward the right wag, you put some weight on the left pole, and vice versa with the wag from right to left—you put some weight on the right pole. This is not a bearing down, but a firm contact with the snow for a slight assist and added stability. (See Figure 92.)

You will find your heel thrust is aided by getting some hip action

Figure 92—Wedeln Exercise in Place

1. Poles firmly planted, skis flat, knees flexed and ready for hop.
2. At the moment of hop, when the heels of the skis are just up off the snow for fanning to the left.
3. End of left fanning movement. Both skis are edged and body is in angulation position, ready for hopping and fanning skis to the right.

behind it. And at this point you will notice something most interesting. In making these arcs from side to side rapidly, you will notice that your body naturally assumes a slight sideward curvature, the so-called "comma position," i.e., angulation, which is perfectly natural and will come to you automatically when you wedel. It is the forced and self-conscious exaggeration of this position which is effected by extremists and which those new to this maneuver find so awkward and difficult.

You will notice something else when you wedel in place. That is that the shoulders play virtually no part in the execution of the maneuver. But please note that word "virtually." Shoulder action is definitely there in wedeln, though it is extremely confined and, one might say, fractional; but the principles of shoulder action and circular motion which have been stressed throughout this book still have their place (in a miniaturized form) in wedeln—and in the same way. If you have not already heard it, you will probably soon hear that reverse shoulder action is required in wedeln. It is our belief that this is the opposite of the case—a subject fully covered in Chapter XIV: "Final Thoughts on Schools of Skiing and the Dynamics of the Art." For the correct touch-timing and instantaneous support that the pole provides, the confined but correct shoulder action is essential.

From Snowplow to Wedeln

An example of what we mean when we iterate and reiterate that every learning-step and maneuver in this book—starting with the most elementary—has direct bearing on the ultimate development of expertness and versatility in the shortest possible time, is the way in which you can use those good old snowplow maneuvers to achieve wedeln action in motion. Find a relatively smooth practice slope of easy gradient, start down in normal schuss position, then—before you attain too much speed to do it in comfort—start rhythmic snowplow turns, linking them with no traverses between.

When you feel you're ready to try converting a snowplow turn into a wedeln turn in the opposite direction, do this: Immediately before your snowplow turn comes around to the position of maximum circular motion, plant the leading pole and lift with vigor as you go into the opposite turn—enough vigor to stroke the relatively weightless inside ski's heel so that the ski is swung parallel to the other ski. The turn made thus is rather abrupt and is done quickly, requiring an almost automatically producing angulation and sharp edging which, later on, when you really wedel, will provide you with the necessary platform that, with the help of the planted pole, is the basis for a wedeln fanning in the opposite direction. Make firm use of the poles to help in lift, weight shift and timing. Each time you shift your weight, plant your pole, always the inside pole, as you turn. We know of no faster, better way to develop the correct pole work for fast wedeln. In fact, if you make your snowplow V smaller and smaller, and your linked turns faster and faster and shorter and shorter, you will be very close to wedeln already. All it needs is to sling the skis, tails only, parallel and together, instead of in the snowplow V.

A modicum of practice in going from plow to wedeln should lead to a real feel for the wedeln motion, and will yield dividends accordingly when you commence to wedel your way down an entire slope at greater speeds.

Study Figure 93; note that forceful pole work virtually buries the snow ring, and that platform and angulation bear close relationship to the hook (page 138).

Figure 93—Wedeln Exercise: Converting Rhythmically Linked Snowplow Turns into Wedeln

1. In snowplow position, the skier—using full knee-and-arm motion—has advanced his right pole to commence right turn.
2. Continuing his rhythmic snowplow turns, skier is now at the moment when left pole is advanced in preparation for left turn.
3. At the end of preceding turn skier firmly plants right pole, and with vigorous lift is ready to swing right ski heel across the snow so that it will be parallel with left ski.
4. The snowplow turns have merged into elementary wedeln.
5. Angulation, edging, pole planting—all lead to natural execution of linked wedeln in opposite direction.

Figure 94—Wedeln Exercise, Straight Run

1. Advancing right pole for placing in snow.
2. Pole has been planted and wedeln is initiated.
3. Lift and fanning of heels of skis. Note angulation of body to get hips lined up with sharply edged skis.

If you had the determination and the physical strength to practice the pre-wedeln exercise in place, and then learned how to convert snowplow turns into wedeln, you are now ready to try another excellent exercise in preparation for the proper use of wedeln. This is practicing wedeln during a straight run on a hard-packed and fairly gentle practice slope, which will give you an opportunity to try the wagging of the skis and the use of poles for exact timing without being distracted by the need to negotiate a difficult slope. Thus you will be able to practice in almost slow motion, you will be able to practice getting up speed in the wagging, and you will discover that the slower the wedeln, the wider the sweeps of the heels of the skis (which tend to delay and restrict the action of the upper body and even leave it behind—with consequent intimations of reverse shoulder). This delay will vanish by the time you are able to wag pretty quickly, with good timing, in the more advanced wedeln.

Before getting on to the straight-run wedeln exercise, some further words about hand and arm position are required. In wedeln, both arms are held forward of the body. The elbows are kept flexed. This is important. If in reaching out to plant the pole near the tip of the ski you extend your arm (like a boxer jabbing), or if you pendulum the pole to get its tip forward, you will throw off your timing and work your weight back on your skis. Whereas if the entire arm is used in advancing the pole, you will have the correct forward arcing of the outside arm, hand and pole necessary to wedel correctly.

In the wedeln you need not worry about the removal of the pole from the snow when it is time to bring it forward. The timing is so fast and the motion is so rhythmical that the waggings and the pole placings interflow—the pole, whose weight has just been relieved, naturally leaves the snow as the arm on that side comes forward.

Of all the ski maneuvers, wedeln puts most emphasis on leg action and pelvis action. *Comparatively* speaking, shoulder motion is non-existent. But the principle of having the outside hand and arm moving with the outside ski remains unaltered.

Learning to wedel during a straight run from schuss position will be easier than it was to learn the snowplow-to-wedeln evolution, although that was essential for its slower motions, during which much was assimilated. On your smooth, rather packed practice slope, schuss normally, then advance and plant the pole firmly enough to aid your lift in unweighting your skis sufficiently so that you can fan the heels, parallel, and then—as your weight returns to the skis with enough angulation to permit sharp edging and the consequent creation of a platform—advance and plant the other pole and take off from your platform with firm thrust in the opposite direction. Figure 94 shows the first half of what we've just described, i.e., the skier executes one wedeln "fan" to the left, from schuss position.

Wedeln from a Traverse

In practicing the ski and body motions of wedeln from a shallow traverse, you are again advised to pick a fairly gentle slope where your speed in the traverse will be rather uniform, and one free of ruts and bumps. This is because the traverse adds a new element to wedeln exercises: lack of symmetry. That is, the wedeln-fanning of the skis uphill (toward the slope) will differ in degree of angulation and amount of thrust from the angulation and thrust required to fan the heels of the skis downslope. It is best, therefore, to start out with a shallow traverse and execute only the downslope fanning, then returning to traverse. Do this several times on each traversing descent until you feel ready to try uphill fanning too. But don't attempt the uphill fanning from the traverse position; you'll be far more successful if you thrust off from the platform that you've created from a previous downhill fanning. With time and practice (not too much of either) you will be able to wag the heels of your skis from side to side of your traverse.

Iselin illustrates the correct way to wedel during a shallow traverse in Figures 95 and 96. The captions provide a step-by-step analysis.

These four wedeln preliminaries—wedeln in place, wedeln emanat-

Figure 95—Wedeln Exercise, Shallow Traverse (*seen from the front*)

1. Traverse and prepare for pole planting.
2. Pole is planted; lift and angulating hip motion will be initiated at this moment.
3. End of heel fanning. Note edged skis and angulation. Skier is already advancing pole for planting it and fanning skis in opposite direction.

The three phases shown correspond exactly to those in Figure 95.

Figure 96—Wedeln Exercise, Shallow Traverse (*as seen from the rear*)

ing from linked snowplow turns, wedeln in a straight run, and wedeln in a shallow traverse—cover the main phases of the finished maneuver. Having learned them, you should be completely ready to try real wedeln. But here again, we wish to stress our belief that it takes a skier who is at least the master of the basic christiania, and is beginning to ski parallel, to properly execute the wedeln. Undoubtedly there are those who have learned it at an earlier phase in their development. Just as surely, there are those who go through a maneuver which they believe to be wedeln and which is not. Undoubtedly there may be some talented teachers who can teach wedeln before the point at which we believe it should be learned. But it is our conviction that, for the vast majority of skiers, this is a maneuver suitable only for the advanced skier.

After that digression, you may be ready for a final maneuver to get you all set for learning and executing the wedeln turns. Note that we do not call this an exercise. There are two reasons for that: first is the fact that what we are about to describe *is* genuine wedeln. Second is the fact that the very word "exercise" gets to be a drag and makes one wonder when the exercises will stop and the fun will begin. So try this next maneuver—it's fun—and bear in mind that all the exercises have led you onward past the point of greatest drudgery and right to the threshold of maximum enjoyment of skiing.

Double-Pole Wedeln on Gentle Slope

Let's get back to that gentle slope. You're going to wend your way a-wedeling right down it, using both your poles in tandem for stability and support, exactly the way you did in that tiresome and tiring exercise called wedeln in place (which is to real wedeling what treading water is to swimming). So, as you can see, that exercise is already coming in handy, just as your gentle-slope, double-pole wedeln training will come in handy at some future date when you're careening down a steep and brutally battered ski run and the going gets really hairy.

Back to the gentle slope, please. Start down in a schuss. Advance and plant both poles simultaneously and far enough forward so you'll have their support while you fan the heels of the skis in one direction. Now, before your bindings get too far past your poles—which would result in your weight being thrown too far back and in loss of timing—and just before you angulate and edge at the end of the fan, advance and plant the poles again, so that you can hop with their help into a fanning in the opposite direction. Repeat. And repeat. And keep your ski tips as close to the fall line as you can while the heels (close and parallel) fan from side to side. And study Figure 97. And try it again. Good! Now you're *really* ready to wedel.

Basic (Recreational) Wedeln

The dynamics of wedeln depend on precise control of body weight. Once this is understood, one can cut through a great deal of the obscure language which so frequently is used about wedeln—to the ultimate frustration of the skier. A simple formulation of this matter of weight control is as follows: The wider the arc of the fan, the more the body's weight must be on the heels. The shorter this fan or arc, the farther forward the weight must come. Finally, in the snake—or serpentine—wedeln down the fall line, with short, extremely rapid arcs, the entire aspect of the body is forward. This is the position in

Figure 97—Double-Pole Wedeln on Gentle Slope

1. Both poles planted; skis are fanned to the right.
2. Hop.
3. Skis fan to the left; note ski edging, angulation, poles in position for planting.
4. Plant poles and hop to right.
5. End of fanning heels to the right, i.e., wedeln to the left. Skier is now ready to hop and fan heels of skis to the left for wedeln to the right.

which rapid and precise pole work is required. It is also the only position that makes it possible to rapidly fan the tails of the skis from side to side while the tips remain in the fall line. Its analogue in nature is the motion of a trout's tail as he keeps himself steady and in line with the current in a brook. A sport analogue is to be found in the art of fencing. The expert fencer keeps the tip of his foil pointed at its target (just as the ski tips stay in the fall line), while his wrist and arm motions rapidly move the hilt of the foil up and down and from side to side in the rapid arcs of parry (just as the ski heels fan rapidly from side to side).

Now let's try a few wedeln turns. Select a sufficiently easy slope so that you can keep your skis pretty much in the fall line without being afraid of picking up so much speed that they will run away from you. Although the major purpose of your wedeln will be to ski the fall line on bumpy slopes, for your first turns you will want to have a smooth slope so that you can perfect your wedeln technique before subjecting it to the test of skiing among moguls. Let's start out with a turn to the right. Your skis are in a traverse position close to the fall line. Arm-and-pole position is forward in preparation for the actual pole work. Knees are elastic and springy, ready to kick off the first turn. You don't need a great deal of speed for this and subsequent early tries. Now, when you are ready to make your right turn, wedeln style, crouch slightly, place the right pole in the snow opposite the shovel and about one foot to the side of it, lift sharply and quickly to arc your parallel ski ends over to the left; simultaneously, the left arm and hand come around with the pole to be planted for the left turn that you will be linking to the right turn. At the end of the arc to the left, edge sharply and energetically, thus providing yourself the springboard platform for the fanning of the skis in the opposite direction for the coming left turn. Ideally (and you'll soon attain this ideal) there is no pause at the ends of the arcs; the biting in of the edges—and pole placement—are immediately followed by the lifting take-off for the fan of the tails of the skis in the opposite direction.

Now let's suppose that you've made two wedeln turns, linked, one to the right and one to the left. How do you account for the fact that they did not work too well? (We can be pretty sure that they didn't—don't be discouraged, they never do at first.) Probably your trouble was somewhat as follows: Most likely the skis picked up too much speed and you found yourself "hanging back"—resulting in, among other things, too much weight on the heels of your skis. Why did the skis pick up this extra speed? Because you didn't make your arcs wide enough. And why didn't you arc more with the back ends of the skis? Because your angulated edging, which was to provide you the strong platform for the take-off was not strong enough to give you the rapid impetus required to swing a sufficient arc. Thus, your arcs too were short and feeble and the skis picked up speed. You may well ask why

the increased speed defeated the wedeln turns that you first tried. The answer is that in all likelihood you were unable to have your pole-timing keep pace with the increased speed. A characteristic of wedeln is that the faster the skier's motion down the slope, the faster the pole movement must be. This facility in pole action and timing must be learned gradually, building up speed as you go. The minute the timing of the pole action falls behind the execution of the wedeln, the skis get ahead of the skier and he is defeated.

Don't be daunted, let's try again. But first study Figures 98 and 99, and read the caption analysis of the five phases shown.

Traverse, elastic knee motion, slight crouch and pole-planting, kick-lift to bring tail ends of the skis to the left, edge hard at the end of the arc, left arm and pole follow the arc motion of the skis and the left pole is planted, kick-lift again and the skis swing to the right—*Oops!* What happened? Something obviously went wrong; most likely what you did was *jump* the ends of your skis. The skis must not leave the snow; the motion must be smooth, with each phase interflowing with the next. Jumping the tails of the skis yields a hard and jerky performance which has very little to do with the timing and beauty of wedeln and throws the skier off balance.

So, let's try yet again. But before we do, let us tell you something about your appearance when you made your more successful second attempt. Believe it or not, at the moment when you applied the hard, sharp, instantaneous edging that is so necessary, you unconsciously "kinked" your knees toward the slope and thereby attained, without trying, the correct angulation. It is our assertion that to consciously strive for this so-called comma position without understanding its dynamics, or realizing why the body naturally assumes it, has nothing to do with the learning of good controlled wedeln skiing. The outcome of such conscious striving is an artificial and superficial resemblance to the real thing. As with most artificial substitutes, the resemblance stops short of results.

Now that we've had this clarification of the comma position, let's get back to another attempt at the correct wedeln. This time, try a

Figure 98—The Basic (Recreational) Wedeln for the Weekend Skier—Employing Heel Thrust on Gentle Slopes

1. Ready for heel thrust to the left, to initiate right turn.
2. Lift to initiate fanning to the left for right turn.
3. Maximum heel thrust.
4. Midpoint of wedeln, just prior to heel thrust to the right for left wedeln.
5. Maximum heel thrust and edging to the left, for right wedeln. Note angulation and that outside hand is in position for planting pole for wedeln in opposite direction.

cadenced counting out loud. If this embarrasses you, count to yourself. The purpose of the count is to give the turns that elastic rhythm and precision of timing which characterize wedeln as done by experts. Count "ONE-*and*-TWO." Like this: ONE (crouch, plant pole) *and* (arc skis), TWO (edge sharply, plant other pole). Don't stop. Keep going ONE-*and*-TWO, ONE-*and*-TWO, ONE-*and*-TWO. Get the rhythm, make your motions precise but fluidly joined and not jerky. The whole body is expressive, as in dancing. When you get up speed, you'll find a better count for you is to omit the *and* and use only the One-Two, One-Two, One-Two.

Figure 99—The Basic (Recreational) Wedeln (*seen from the rear, going away from camera*). The phases of the maneuver shown correspond to those in Figure 98.

An Important Digression

Now let's take time out (while you catch your breath) for another important digression into the dynamics of wedeln. Again, our purpose will be to clarify what has too often become obscured. If, as we urged earlier, you do not attempt to learn wedeln until you have achieved the basic christie or parallel-skiing stage, then—automatically and unconsciously—you will be advancing the inside ski in the wedeln turns without thinking about it. It is inconceivable to us that anyone who has progressed even as far as a fair basic christie will not automatically advance the inside ski of a turn; it should be an integral part of his technique, done without thinking. However—and this is important—it sometimes happens that well-meant but short-cut instruction in wedeln perforce focuses attention on the importance of advancing the inside ski. This can have most unfortunate results: the skier becomes self-conscious about leading with the inside ski, so he actually thrusts it forward. Simple physics tells us that the countereffect, i.e., the reaction to this action, is to throw the body back. The natural and automatic advancing of the inside ski (about three inches) is correct and permits the continued forward aspect of the body so necessary to wedeln timing. The conscious thrusting forward of the inside ski *too far* sets the body back, throws off the timing, ruins stability and leads to failure. You may have the greatest intellect and the fastest reaction time in the world, but if you have to ski with your brain instead of with a body by now possessed of trained reflexes, you have built-in problems which may well prove insurmountable.

In this connection, we might point out that since every isolated motion in skiing must be a smooth-flowing part of an integrated whole, so an error in any one phase leads to other errors in the whole. Here is how this interdependence can work against you through the making of one error. The thrusting forward too far of the inside ski puts the skier's weight so far back that he can't unweight the heels sufficiently for correct fanning. The result is that the skier must jump in order to unweight the backs of the skis enough for fanning. We have been stressing the importance of pole work and timing. We would like to stress it again—it is virtually impossible to overstress it—and would like to point out that the forward aspect of the body and forward motion are essential for correct pole work and the critical timing it requires. This is one of the secrets of correct wedeln. Without it, you will be unable to wedel through bumps. Without it, you will also have to think about the weighting of the outside ski instead of having this happen automatically.

Apropos pole work: you will find, as your wedeln is perfected, that the speed you're going determines, to a degree, the placing of the pole. In a fast wedeln, the pole tip enters the snow as far forward as the tip of the ski; in a slow wedeln, you may find the correct pole position somewhere between the tip and the binding. In a fast wedeln the pole will automatically be out of the snow and starting forward again before the binding catches up with it, or right at the binding; in the slower wedeln, the pole tip will leave the snow somewhat later.

Now a final word about basic, recreational wedeln—and why we call it both recreational and basic. It is basic in that it provides the foundation for the very fast, expert, perfectly timed and beautifully fluid high-speed wedeln. It is recreational in the sense that it's fun and not too hard to do, and is therefore most suitable for the occasional or weekend skier who wants to add wedeln to his repertory, yet does not have the time or the timing (or, let's face it—perhaps the courage) to take his wedeln much further. Let us stress again, too, a few of the distinguishing characteristics of this recreational-yet-basic maneuver, and then point out one *visual* pitfall of which a few rather "other-directed" skiers are not fully aware.

In recreational wedeln, the arcs of the tails of the skis are quite wide, with consequent dependence on great heel thrust, which in turn puts the skier's weight a bit back on his skis, since this is the only way to really achieve the heel thrust required. There is also a distinct hesitation—in fact, it can properly be described as a pause—between the arcs, as opposed to the expert wedeln in which the side-to-side motion of the heels is flowingly continuous, with very sharp edging and angulation at the ends of the arcs. It sometimes happens that, in order to achieve the proper heel thrust and to permit this pause at the ends of the arcs, the skier must maintain his equilibrium by falling so far behind in his timing that circular motion gives way to reverse motion, as compensation for the rhythm-interrupting pauses at the ends of the arcs. When this is done intentionally, exaggerated, and in the mistaken belief that it is a joy for all to behold such grace, the skier has the appearance of seeming to swish down the slope in a mincing manner, his pelvis thrust seductively forward and twitching from side to side—with a result that is positively adorable and may lead the innocent bystander to wonder why the wedeler isn't carrying his purse. (It's only fair to add that on attractive women this terpsichorean twisting often looks fine.)

Wedeln for Rough Terrain

Once you have mastered wedeln on smooth slopes and have become proficient in the rapid and precise timing and the elasticity of movement required, you are ready to employ wedeln in negotiating the terrain for which it was invented. We might repeat here that to wedel on a smooth slope of not too steep grade can be done for fun and amusement—but it is not necessary. It is when the expert skier wants to negotiate a downhill run which is studded with moguls that wedeln comes into its own. The fall line is his ideal course. Since the fall line is only *theoretically* straight, the exact following of it through moguls is, of course, impossible. It is the aim of the skier who wedels to select and negotiate the straightest possible course down the slope, thus achieving the closest practical approximation to skiing the fall line. (See Figure 100.)

How is this done? You will recall that we have been talking continually about the importance of making a pre-evaluation of the possible course before taking off. For the expert skier, this is an automatic part of his repertory; he looks at the slope and instantly analyzes the opportunities it offers for rapid descent under control.

The basic-christie skier, skiing among moguls, follows the grooves. The parallel skier uses the lower parts of the walls of the grooves to bank his turns. The skier who wedels also follows the grooves, but he may fling the tails of the skis against the side walls to check his speed should he need to. Usually, however, he does his checking in those brief instants when one groove opens out just before the next one begins.

In skiing among moguls and at high speed, the skier who wedels seems to dart rather than turn. His motion is less that of a swooping bird and more like the trout we talked about earlier, who can, through rhythmic movements of his tail, maintain his place in a fast current or dart from side to side. The skier who knows wedeln shows prodigious speed and timing in the rapidity of the tail-wagging of his skis and the placement of his poles. He does not have time to hesitate in his choice of course. His decisions are made instantaneously—he employs his wedeln for maneuvering rather than for checking. Skiers themselves, in talking about this attitude of total readiness and split-second timing, frequently use a German word, *wendig*, which we might approximate with the English words, "flexible," "maneuverable," or the notion of optimum movement. The aim is speed; the means to it is a fluid and flexible control which permits the skier to exploit every variation in terrain, every alternation in possible course, every dip and leveling in gradient to impel him faster and closer to the fall line.

Of course, not all skiers who wedel always want to see how fast they can get down a mogul-studded slope. If they wish, they can make traverses; frequently they will keep the tips of the skis in a groove and fan the heels somewhat up the side wall to check speed. In such circumstances wedeln might be likened to the constant (though confined) movement of the steering wheel of a car, which is the mark of the good driver who employs this means to compensate for unevennesses and to have the feel of the car continuously in his hands—instead of just holding the wheel rigid and letting the car run, employing the steering wheel only for actual turns. Thus it will be seen that wedeln is not only a means of turning and of checking speed, but is, perhaps most importantly, a means whereby the skier is in constant intimate touch with the terrain—rough or smooth—over which he is skiing.

Figure 100—Use of Wedeln for Skiing Rough and Bumpy Terrain

1. Ready to lift and fan heels to the right.
2. Lifted position and fanning of heels of skis.
3. Full heel thrust to the right and body and pole prepared for initiating wedeln in opposite direction.
4. Pole planted and heels of skis beginning to fan to the left for right wedeln.
5. In midturn, note sharp edging, angulation, and forward circular motion of outside arm and shoulder.

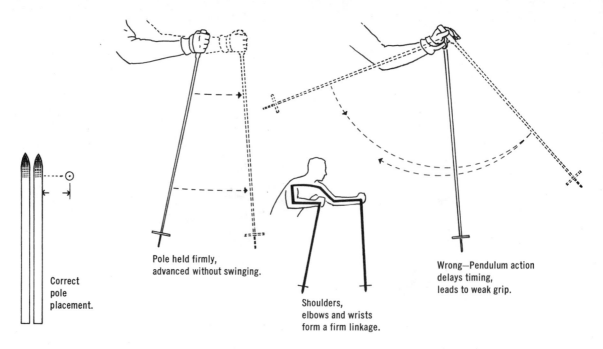

Correct pole placement.

Pole held firmly, advanced without swinging.

Shoulders, elbows and wrists form a firm linkage.

Wrong—Pendulum action delays timing, leads to weak grip.

Figure 101—Pole Work in Short Swings and Wedeln

High-Speed and Serpentine (Snake) Wedeln

It is in the very rapid wedeln close to the fall line, or in a high-speed steep traverse, that the skier who has learned his wedeln with good forward aspect of the body will appreciate the time and attention he gave to learning it. For now he can do the rapid arcing of the skis with very little effort, the ski heels being virtually weightless, thanks to his forward stance. Of course when the skier who wedels slings the backs of his skis against the walls of a groove to check his speed, he weights them sufficiently to achieve the braking motion. But as soon as the desired braking is thus achieved, his weight comes forward again where it must be in order to give him the weightless tails and the rapid pole work which distinguish good, fast wedeln.

The ultimate in high-speed wedeln is what we call the snake wedeln, and is graphically described in the French word *serpentine*. Study Figure 102 and the step-by-step captioning of it. This is the serpentine or snake wedeln seen in a series of stop-action photographs taken split seconds apart. The skier is in a situation of constant anticipation, that is, he is above and even a bit ahead of his skis at all times, and he employs extreme fluidity of motion and far-forward circular motion so that he will be in total control of the rapidly moving skis, while the heels of the skis are thus permitted to fan rapidly from side to side. The constant forward pressure and extremely rapid pole work—the fact that the skier is virtually diving ahead while the heels of his skis fan in short arcs from side to side—make it virtually impossible to sustain the serpentine for a long stretch, especially through bumpy terrain. The serpentine wedeler anticipates when it is essential to check his speed; he does so by applying a stronger arc, extremely quickly and briefly, and just enough to re-establish total control for the

8.

launching of a new series of serpentine wedels. No one can say how often or how sharply the speed will be checked, since this depends on a combination of factors which not only depend upon the skier's skill and timing speed, but also on the steepness of the terrain and variations in it. We refer you to Figure 102 which shows the dynamic and constant forward drive that characterizes this maneuver.

Some pages back we talked about the prima donna of the slopes who would prefer to fall in perfect form rather than continue skiing and commit some momentary awkwardness. In the rapid negotiation of bumpy terrain close to the fall line, the true expert will quite naturally

Figure 102—High-Speed or Snake Wedeln

1. High-speed attack with skier in continuous fluid and forceful forward motion, which includes anticipatory forward movement of ouside shoulder and pole.
2. Demonstrating rapid and anticipatory pole motion. Note that outside pole is ready to be planted while inside pole is still coming up out of the snow.
3. With the skier's motion always forward, the pole is planted and the heels of the skis are free to fan easily and rapidly.
4. There is no pause midway in the turn; the skier continues to press forward and use vigorous, extremely rapid action of the body and arms to stay above and very much with the skis.
5. Again, the skier's body and pole action are almost ahead of the skis as he constantly drives forward, well above his skis, rather than letting them overrun him to the slightest degree, which would result in a slowing and weighting of the heels.
6. Again, note anticipatory and rapid pole placement and forward body position to facilitate fanning of the heels of the skis and to keep the skier well above the forward part of the skis.
7. Rapid and fluid lift plus anticipatory forward drive of outside shoulder and arm assure that the skier will be leading his skis into these rapid maneuvers, rather than following them.
8. Dynamic forward drive of the snake wedeln assures total control without lessening speed.

swing his poles and his arms into postures and positions which—when caught by a stop-motion camera—seem to reveal poor form. Actually, it is the mark of good form to be flexible enough and elastic enough to make these instantaneously corrective motions. It is not infrequent for an expert skier to use two poles rather than one for that stabilizing instant at the launching of a turn or the initiation of a maneuver. (This, you will remember, we showed in Figure 86.) Certainly, in taking off for the prejump over a sharp drop, two poles can be very helpful. Two poles may also be employed in taking off in the airplane turn. In any case, the strong likelihood is that the well-trained skier who has a reasonable and logical technique will not have to worry too much about his form (in the "formal" sense) because it will be an integral part of everything he does on the slope.

Short Swing

What we will call the short swing is an important high-speed maneuver, wherein the skier employs the same kind of anticipation and "being ahead of his skis" that he uses in the snake wedeln. The purpose is the same: to stay a bit ahead of and on top of the skis, and to maintain vigorous and forward body motion and forward circular motion in order to sustain speed while making tight turns. This is accomplished by keeping the heels of the skis free to fan from side to side without risking the loss of control through falling behind the

---

Figure 103—The Short Swing with Anticipation

1. As the skier approaches the turning place, he anticipates the turn itself with vigorous lift, forward circular motion, and a consequent weightlessness of the heels of the skis.
2. As the skier goes into his sharp turn, it may be seen that the anticipatory movements of No. 1 (*above*) have made it possible for him to stay above and forward on his skis while the heels arc forcefully and quickly in a very short radius.
3. Angulation and continuous forward circular body motion make it possible for the skier to carve out a short-radius, high-speed controlled swing, leaving him in correct anticipatory position for a short swing in the opposite direction without loss of speed or timing.
4. Still ahead of his skis, still anticipating their movement (and hence guiding it), the skier launches directly into the next short swing in the opposite direction.
5. End phase of short swing, showing readiness for the next swing: sharp edging, forward body position, the angulation necessary to firmly carve the turn and control the sharply edged skis.

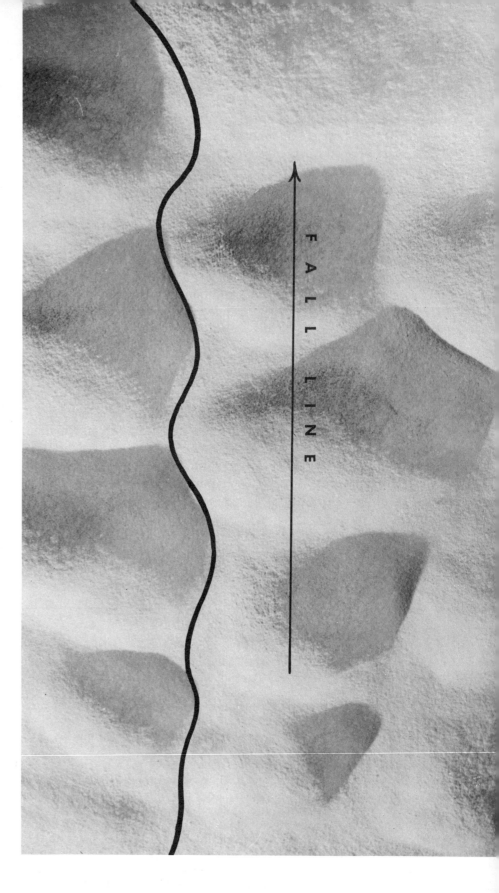

Figure 104—Wedeln Among Bumps, Close to Fall Line

skis in order to attain vigorous heel thrust. In other words, with the weight well forward and the skier's body movements constantly anticipating the movements of the skis, it is possible to so unweight the heels that they will easily fan from side to side in response to the skier's forward body movement, instead of requiring employment of the leg muscles in thrusting them from side to side.

The short swing is really a very tight and almost abrupt turn, although the word "abrupt" must not be understood to have any implications of arresting the smooth flow of fast descent. The wedeln movements in the short swing are somewhat modified, since what is wanted is rapid turning without diminution of speed, although the maneuver may be used to check speed if that is desired. The correct execution of the short swing is shown in Figure 103. Note the thrust and expressiveness of the skier's entire body in executing the short swing.

Your wedeln repertory is now complete: Proper employment of the wedeln for rough terrain, the serpentine wedeln, and the short swing will make it possible for you to descend a steep and mogul-studded rough run as shown in Figure 104.

And now we'll get to two maneuvers that are nonessentials, but that can give you a lot of pleasure and no little admiration.

Two Maneuvers Just for Kicks— the Mambo and the Reuel Swing

Someday, when you're feeling full of beans and find yourself with a nice smooth slope that isn't too steep, you may want to try to mambo on skis—a spectacular-looking maneuver that is totally unsuitable as a method of negotiating normally difficult or high-speed conditions. You will recall that when you were first learning wedeln, making rather wide arcs, your timing tended to get out of phase with your skis and thus reverse shoulder action ensued. In doing the mambo, your skis and your body motion are intentionally and completely out of phase, so the reverse shoulder action is extreme. It helps to flail away with your poles, letting them swing freely as you rotate your shoulders away from the direction of turning. You'll have to swing your hips out of line with your body, so that you can bring the weight over the outside ski, and this is a position in which it is extremely easy to trip the edges. That's just one reason this maneuver is not suitable for rough terrain. Your edging and angulation will also have to be extreme enough to compensate for the reverse shoulder action, or you may skid completely out of control. But done with spirit and abandon, and with appropriately tropical enthusiasm and rhythm, the mambo can make you look and feel like a happy expert having a ball. Figures 105 and 106 show how it's done. (We'll have a lot more to say on the serious side about mambo-style wedeln in Chapter XIV.)

Figure 105—The Mambo Wedeln (*seen from the front*)

The Reuel turn, or Reuel swing, is a quite acrobatic and useless (though spectacular) maneuver. It is sometimes mistakenly called the Royal turn, but this is incorrect: it has nothing to do with royalty whatever, but was named after a Mr. Reuel, who evolved an entire technique based on skiing on one ski as much as possible. It is, in essence, an extreme form of downhill skating step, prolonged and shaped into a full curve on one ski. Figure 107 shows how it's done. We suggest that you practice it in private before displaying it in public, unless you're doing it for laughs rather than for admiration. Some beginners and intermediate skiers have been known to perform a Reuel turn unintentionally, thanks to skiing off-balance and stiff-legged, and thus being tipped onto one ski while the other ski is practically held aloft as a counterbalance that will hopefully restore the skier to the vertical. This is good for laughs, too, for the short space of time it takes the skier to give up and nestle down in the snow horizontally.

As we've said, properly executed, the mambo wedeln and the Reuel turn can be spectacular good fun. No one (with the exception of the aforementioned Mr. Reuel) would think of restricting his maneuvering to Reuel turns; unhappily, the same can't be said of the mambo wedeln, which some misguided people seem to think is the only and ultimate way to descend a ski slope. Alas for them: they don't know, as you now do, the tremendous thrills and pleasures to be gained from a full and fully developed repertory of skiing maneuvers that liberates the accomplished skier from thinking about his skis, and leaves him free to soar on the mountain as a bird soars in flight.

Figure 106—The Mambo Wedeln (*seen from the rear, going away from camera.*)

Figure 107—The Reuel Turn

1. Skier approaches skate-off point.
2. Strong forward and upward projection of body from flat inside ski which is being guided in the direction of the turn. Outside ski is leaving the snow.
3. At midturn, skier is sharply banked, inside ski edged, arms in airplane-wing position. Centrifugal force helps keep outside ski in air; it is not brought forward but comes around by itself as skier continues to turn.
4. Two-thirds through the turn, the body is still erect and banking sharply to maintain equilibrium on one ski.
5. The turn is virtually completed as the outside ski descends toward the snow, parallel to the inside ski.
6. Ski-out position, after the turn, solid on both skis again, the knees having been flexed to absorb the landing.

CHAPTER TWELVE

YOU ON A DOWNHILL RUN

The following is not, in the direct sense, a chapter of instruction. It is included here so that those interested—and any doubting Thomases —can go through a ski run on paper and see how everything taught in this book is of practical value and of importance to the all-round skier. Here, too, you will find hints and reminders, and, we hope, a little of the thrill of skiing.

It's a grand day, clear and cold but not too cold; there is no wind, and you're up early, properly dressed for skiing, breakfasted and (we hope) feeling fine after a good night of sound sleep. So out you come, with your skis over your shoulder, and off you go to the ski slopes.

Today is the day you've been planning for so long, the day you go up to the top of the mountain, higher than the lift will take you—and then down all the way, down the schusses and down the trails, down through the trees and over the open spaces, down, down, down until you come to the final schuss and the end of a marvelous run—you hope. And since we can foresee the future (on this day, anyway) we'll tell you your hopes are going to be realized.

You are at the lift, with your lift ticket punched. Get in line (or are you the first out today?) and when you get to the starting line wait for the chair to come around. Sit as it touches you, grasp the upright, keep your poles clear and your ski tips up. . . . The snowscape unfolds as you ride upward, and soon you approach the top of the lift. Get set, and as the snow comes up under your skis, rise and ski away.

You walk on the level with fine, reaching parallel strides, over to the rope tow, which goes even higher than the lift. In line again; poles correctly held, skis parallel, you grasp the rope and with flexed arms taking up the shock of starting you're off and upward bound again. At the top of the tow you let go neatly, ski out of the way of those coming along behind you, step-turn around, and—there, before you, stretched out for miles and miles, going off into incredible distance, you see hills of white.

But the real summit is still above you, so you turn again and start up in good, easy traverses, edging nicely, keeping the body erect, using your poles to help you. As you look down you may feel that instant of panic which makes you want to lean in toward the hill, but you know that's less secure than keeping your body directly above your skis.

Kick turn, and then a traverse in the new direction.

Now you're nearing the top and it's getting a little steeper. Starting your half side steps, you keep forging forward. Now you come to an escarpment, an outcropping of rock which you can skirt, if you wish, but there's a clear path up between two projections of rock, and although it's too narrow for your half side step or traverses, you can make it with the herringbone step.

Pretty tiring, wasn't it? But you don't want to pause, so you proceed up the last few yards with the full side step and now, well, who can describe the sensation of being at the very top of a mountain, with the view unfolded all around you, and the sky stretching blue and limitless above?

While you rest from your climb, you look down and plan your course. Ready? First, adjust the bindings on your skis. For the climb, the cable was in the first side clips. For the trip down you hook it under both clips, getting full downpull on the heels. Bootlaces good and tight? Cap on firmly enough so it won't blow off? Poles held correctly?

You move along your level space at the top until your ski tips hang over the lip, pointing into thin air. You flex your knees, your heart beats faster, you tense for the take-off—and then you give yourself a little lecture: "Take it easy, don't be tense, good springy skiing is what we want."

And then you're off, in a schuss which gathers speed as you go, so that when you come to the path where you did your herringbone, you flash between the rocks.

The rocks behind you, you find you're going mighty fast and heading for a clump of trees. Off to the left, there's more clear slope. A fast christie swings you into a traverse. Now you're angling down, skis parallel, standing easily and comfortably on your skis, but alertly, and with your skis equally edged and close together.

As you approach the open slope, you can see more and more of it. Hmm, seems pretty steep. Better have a good look at the whole expanse before attempting it. Another stem christie, sharper than the first, slows you down some, and then you prepare and execute, by Ullr, a perfect stop christie.

Mighty steep slope we're looking down, you and we over your shoulder. You wonder what's around the clump of pines on the edge of the slope, halfway down. Can't quite see around them, and you don't want to ski down slowly for a look, because that would be wasting a fine schuss. How about risking a schuss anyway? Not you; you're a safe and sensible skier.

So you sideslip down the steep start of the slope for a bit, and then edge to a stop. Going straight down those few feet gives you the view you want—there's a wide trail leading off at an angle from the slope, through a patch of woods. Looks interesting.

You get set to go down the open slope. You figure three wide swings will serve the double purpose of controlling your speed and heading you into the trail on the last traverse.

Off you go, traverses linked with christies, and a feeling of flying making you smile as you ride. And then you whiz onto the trail and—oops!—there's a bare stump, right in front of you. A quick, neat pole christie, and you're around it safely, and high-balling along.

Now you see that the trail seems to come to an abrupt end up ahead. Looks like pretty thick woods there. A tight, deft stop christie, with good countermotion and sharp lift and swing, brings you to a stop. And now you snowplow forward a few feet, slowly, scanning the trail ahead. Trees, trees, trees. What have you got yourself into? Are you going to have to backtrack uphill and seek another way down? You press down the heels of your skis, bringing your plow to a stop—and then you notice that the trail, which looked as if it were at an end, makes an abrupt turn downhill. Looking ahead and preplanning, you decide on short-swinging your way through the trees.

Now the trail has narrowed too much to permit linking sharp swings to keep your speed down, so you employ your basic wedeln.

The trees get sparser. Off to the right you see that they're petering out at the edge of another open slope. Now you stop wedeling and traverse toward the open. And then, traversing for a bit, you come to the last few trees, and by now you have enough speed to swing in and out of them, as if you were running a slalom, except that it's easier.

Here you are, out of the woods, and dropping away below you is a rolling open slope which gets steeper as it goes. It ends in a level runout, and after the runout there is a slight rise. You feel like letting out a whoop as you turn into the fall line and let 'er rip. The skis pick up speed, and you're right with them, poised squarely over them, knees flexing to take up the bumps in the terrain.

Faster! And faster! The strain on leg and ankle is perceptible now as you schuss down and down, the wind singing in your ears, the skis roaring over the snow. Now, while you still can, you start a series of long-radius parallel swings, crossing back and forth over the fall line, staying close to it, keeping you at uniform speed and giving you the knowledge that you're definitely Superman, at least. At your high speed the long swings are easy, and the rhythm of them and the plume of snow that accompanies you like the bow wave of a ship makes us, who are looking over your shoulder, very proud indeed.

As you approach the bottom of the slope, you point the tips straight down again for a final schuss, and then you flash out onto the level and sail across it, and even, at diminishing speed, up the rise beyond it, using your pure or stop christie to come to a halt on the ridge at its end. Good thing, too, because if you'd been reckless and let yourself go on over the crest without looking, you would have cracked up on an outcropping of rock. Being a good skier, you look before you leap.

Now, looking down a way you see the regular open slope served by the ski lift, off to your left. You see, too, that a knoll which you passed on your way down offers, from its top, a good way to get to the slope, and you decide to climb it.

Two uphill traverses and a tough, short stint of herringboning bring you to the summit of the knoll, and there's a trough-shaped trail running down through the trees to the slope you're heading for. You swing down the easy way, for the shape of the trail, with its upcurving sides, slows you on each traverse as you approach the bordering trees and makes a christie the simplest of matters—and then you traverse down—across the trail again and up the curve of the other side, and another christie starts you across again.

As you near the opening of the slope you schuss down the center of the trail, and then you see ahead of you a patch of rutted, pitted snow, which melted in yesterday's afternoon sun and has since frozen somewhat. You set yourself to ski across it, but as you start you notice a set of slalom flags directly below. It would be fun to run through the gates, you decide, and you want to turn. The rutted snow would make turning hard if it weren't for your skillful pole christie which gives you the tripod action you need for a secure turn under these circumstances.

As you approach the slalom course, you get set and then attempt the supreme test of skill and timing—tight turns and fast pole work as you go through the gates and flushes, every muscle straining to keep speed and yet cross between the pairs of flags.

Well, too bad, you missed one, didn't you? But the foot of the slope is in sight and you spy some friends standing there. A final schuss, and as you approach them you let yourself come nearer and nearer, at full speed. A Reuel turn with a good plume of snow, right in front of them. That should impress them.

Hmm. How in heaven's name did you happen to fall? Of course, you know better than to show off by trying to scare people, but it would have been fun. Well, next time, you decide, you won't be quite so fancy. Anyway, you know how to get up!

So up you get, grin sheepishly, and head for the lift again. One more run is what you're after; it's still early enough, and you haven't had your fill. But this time, you decide, you'll just ski the regular terrain, instead of going off on your own to virgin snow. Which means moguls!

Are you defeated? Not you. You start out on a traverse, bumpy but shallow enough to let you do a bit of planning ahead. You are skiing with good elasticity; your poles are held forward at the ready for stabilizing action, timing, and short swinging. When you find a convenient mogul of just the right size, you ride up it, use its crown to give you lift, use your pole and make a parallel turn into the groove.

Coming out of that groove you've picked up speed. You're closer to the fall line, too. A few parallel turns with poles are now in order. Using the terrain for lift and banking on the walls of grooves, it's easy. Ahead, you see three moguls which are quite steep and close together. You have the speed and the control to use the first for the take-off of an airplane turn—and you land neatly in the groove on the downhill side of the third. As it widens, momentarily, you check a bit with a fast wedeln while you look ahead. Looks good—bumpy but negotiable close to the fall line, thanks to your wedeln technique. So it's wedeln through the rest of the moguls. Then you see that you're approaching a steep drop-off. You can avoid it, but why should you? Gauging your speed and distance, you prejump and are airborne well before you cross its lip—with the result that you land smoothly and gracefully.

The rest of the run is easy because the slope is not too steep and the terrain is smooth. A schuss with a bit of mambo wedeln for control, for fun, and for—well, for the hell of it. Why not—it's been a hell of a fine day! You're just sorry it's over.

It *was* a marvelous run, though, wasn't it? You take off your skis, wipe them dry, put the running surfaces together and lay them over your shoulder. Walking to the inn, you feel the joy of accomplishment and the physical glow of muscles well tried and now relaxed.

And that night, do you boast of your run? Do you drink yourself tipsy? Do you stay up late and devote yourself to the building of a beautiful hangover?

Why not? Unless, of course, you want to ski tomorrow.

CHAPTER THIRTEEN

COMPETITIVE EVENTS

One of the wonderful things about skiing is the nature of ski competition. Unlike many other sports, in which direct competition of one person with another is the rule, or in which brute force is the deciding factor, ski competition is always against time, or against distance, and the skill, ingenuity, courage, and intelligence of the skier determine his chances of success.

Ski races are thrilling to watch, esthetically as well as for the excitement of the competition itself.

Watch a slalom race. A course is laid out on a steep slope. Pairs of flags are arranged in various patterns. The skier must ski through each pair. Lots are drawn for order of starting and the race is on. Tight, split-second turns carry the racer down the course; if he misses a gate of flags with part of a ski, or parts of both skis, he is penalized in terms of seconds added to his total time. Here is the race par excellence to test the art of the skier, who is pitted not against a fellow opponent whom he may outfox or outweigh, but against a tricky course and a stop watch. (A typical slalom course is shown on opposite page. For international competition rules [F.I.S. Rules] write to the National Ski Association of America, 1130 16th Street, Denver, Colorado.)

Or take ski jumping, that glorious and beautiful defiance of gravity. It is not only the distance a man jumps which determines his score; he is rated on form in the descent before the jump, the jump itself, the flight through the air, the landing, the runout. And each point for or against him in his form rating concerns a facet of technique evolved for safe jumping as well as long-distance jumping.

Cross-country racing is less easy on the spectator than slalom and jumping, but it tests to the utmost the all-round skill and stamina of the skier, who must go through wood and glen, across streams, up and down trails, over or around obstacles.

And then there's the downhill race, perhaps the most thrilling of them all. In this, the start and the finish line are marked. Usually the start is at the top of a mountain and the finish at the bottom. The course in between is up to the skier. When he leaves the starting line he must select his way down and his manner of descent. He comes to a steilhang (an extremely steep slope, usually bounded by rocks or trees). Will he try to schuss? If he does, will he be able to negotiate the sharp turn at the bottom of the steilhang? Will his legs stand up to the schuss, if he does select it? And the turns. His speed must be under control, his eyes and muscles ready to take advantage of each dip or bump in the terrain, his brain ready to make instant judgments.

And there are combination races which are the true tests of all-round expertness.

But there is another kind of competition you will be interested in. It is for you. At every ski resort there are class competitions in which you can test your skill and your mettle against time. The spirit of the contestants is serious but never grim; the spectators, if any, cheer for all, and when you've won the bronze pin, or the silver ski, or the lapel button or shoulder patch which tells the world that you made a specific run within a certain time, or maybe some token that shows you did better than anyone else that year, then you know a glow and a thrill and a pleasure which are hard to describe. And how hard and willingly you'll work to do better next time!

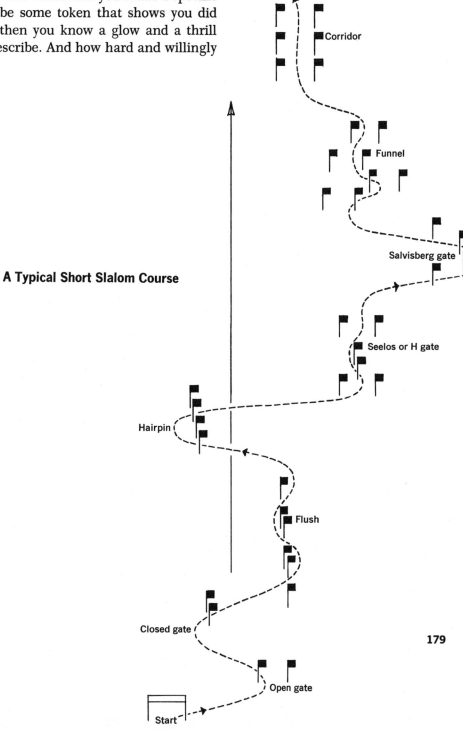

A Typical Short Slalom Course

Corridor

Funnel

Salvisberg gate

Seelos or H gate

Hairpin

Flush

Closed gate

Open gate

Start

CHAPTER FOURTEEN

FINAL THOUGHTS ON SCHOOLS OF SKIING AND THE DYNAMICS OF THE ART

In this book we have repeatedly attempted to make clear our belief that the method of skiing expounded in its pages is scientifically accurate, logical, effective and sound. We have purposely avoided criticizing any other specific method. We have gone out of our way to state that individual skiers have developed their own individual styles and techniques which are immensely effective for them and which can be learned by others—though we've maintained that this is an approach to learning that is unpredictable in outcome. On the other hand, in fairness to the recreational skier, we have pointed out that there exist schools of teaching which develop skiers of sadly limited resources, people who can ski very adequately on packed and smooth slopes but who are defeated by deep snow and rough terrain. These are the people who find themselves helpless in situations approximating Alpine conditions. Not only are they defeated, but they are cheated of the ultimate joy of skiing, which is skiing in the mountains, not on prepared slopes. All this we have stated in one way or another several times throughout this book. Now we must go a step further.

Let us first talk sensibly and without prejudice about reverse shoulder action, recently enjoying a considerable vogue.

Let's forget about skiing entirely for a moment and think about cars. Every driver knows the sickening feeling of the unintentional skid. All race drivers know the feeling of the intentional skid. In either case, the way out of a skid is to steer in the direction of the skid, not away from it. Thus, if in your car you are making a right turn and the rear wheels skid out to the left, you will wind the steering wheel to the left to straighten out the car and establish traction between the wheels and the road again. In automobile racing, there are not infrequent situations wherein an entire turn, especially on a dirt track, is negotiated via a controlled skidding of the rear wheels, while the front wheels are steered in compensation. But there is another kind of racing turn, one that is virtually unknown to the non-racing driver, and that is the drift. Drivers of "formula" race cars—as opposed to stock cars—are very familiar with it. It is an intricate and difficult maneuver that takes extraordinary skill and daring. In essence, drift is achieved when all four wheels of the car are sliding laterally and equally while they continue to roll forward. In drifting around a turn, the attitude of the car is comparable to what it would be if all four wheels were non-steerable and the car was tethered by a cable to the center of the turn, with the cable being the radius of the turn and the car following the circumference. (But please note well: "drift" is a very dirty word among skiers, who—because they can edge their skis and bank with their bodies—carve turns and don't actually drift them. But although drift is therefore a dirty word, the analogy with race driving is valid.)

What has all this got to do with skiing? Simply this: reverse steering is required to compensate for skidding rear wheels, just as reverse shoulder is required to compensate for skidding of the tails of the skis; in normal driving, the steering is normal, just as in normal skiing the circular motion of the body is normal; in high-speed driving, when the car has drifted, steering is present but minimal, just as in high-speed skiing circular motion is present but is not emphasized.

Think about a skier who enters a turn and has the tails of his skis skid beyond the desired degree necessary to carve the turn. What can he do to get the skis back under him and to convert the skid into a turn? The only compensatory movement possible for him is reverse shoulder action. In fact, it is possible (and it has been done) to evolve a technique of skiing which is built entirely on what, in an automobile, would be intentionally skidding at the initiation of a turn and then steering in the direction of the skid to compensate for it. That is, the turn is initiated very hard, with a lot of skidding of the heels of the skis, and reverse shoulder action is employed to compensate for the initial skid. The physics, the dynamics, of correct skiing at high speed are analogous to the drifting of turns in a formula race car, and not to the intentional skidding of only the rear wheels of a car. In skiing at normal speeds, as in driving at normal speeds, normal body motion is employed—not its reverse.

Consider again the analogy of the automobile. Or, rather, try to think of skiing and of car driving simultaneously—and then you can grasp the fact that direct shoulder action approximates the movements of shoulders, elbows and hands in steering a car. When you put your car into a right turn, it is your left arm, elbow, hand that go forward. When you are driving straight, your shoulders are at right angles to the direction of your motion. When you are turning left, it is your right arm and hand that go forward. Similarly, with correct, controlled skiing, the movements of the skier's body are such that he remains directly, firmly and controlledly over his skis—and does not let them leave him behind or slide out from under him sideways.* This *may* happen. It may be that in negotiating a tricky slope or a tricky slalom course the skier will have to contort his body and resort to compensations and overcompensations in the interest of achieving his goal of speed and more speed. (Parenthetically, it may be interesting to speculate here on why, if what we say is true, so many pictures of expert skiers seem to show them in positions and postures other than those we prescribe as correct. The answer is not far to seek: These make the most interesting, unusual and exciting photographs, and photographers are in the business of selling pictures, not teaching skiing. But to use these spectacular and enjoyable pictures as models is not the road to controlled skiing.)

Figures 108A and 108B illustrate the differences between free-form skiing with normal body motion, and the abnormal posture required when a turn of the same radius is shaved close to an obstacle. In Figure 108A you will see that the skier is turning around a small pine bough that is placed in the snow as a marker. He is using normal body motion, is properly banking his turn, and is carving it rather than skidding it. Throughout the turn, his body is above and with his skis, and his shoulders are squarely across them. In Figure 108B one pole of a slalom gate has been driven into the snow right beside the pine bough. The skier is now forced to approach his turn in abnormal position and to tuck in his inside arm and shoulder to clear the pole—with resulting extreme angulation and appearance of intentional reverse shoulder action. Compare the four identical phases of the turns in Figure 108A and Figure 108B and decide for yourself which looks more normal, fluid, natural, pleasurable.

Let us now examine the matter of wedeln. The trend to wedeln—which has become a virtual fad—has done much to advance the cause of reverse shoulder action. Let us now say something about that.

As we have pointed out, there are two distinct forms of wedeln: wedeln with a purpose, and wedeln for fun—which has little value in terms of technique. About the latter, we need say nothing; if you enjoy it, more power to you. About wedeln with a purpose, Iselin speaks as follows: "During past seasons we had the pleasure of watching international skiers of the highest caliber skiing in Aspen. These men were observed closely, not only when training for races and in actual slalom and downhill racing, but when skiing among themselves on

---

* The exact synchronization of all body and ski motions is a critical concern for the elite skier. Specifically, he is faced with the problem of synchronizing body motion with the very rapid arcing of the tails of his skis, in order to be "with" and "above" them at all times. This is not always possible; it happens from time to time that the leg motion outpaces the motion of the upper body, timing is lost, and reverse (delayed) shoulder action results. Top skiers who find their timing is off in this way will usually slow down the arcing of their skis a bit until they get back into correct timing—thus regaining the much-needed stability which only correct timing affords.

Aspen Mountain for fun. While skiing among themselves, reverse shoulder action was virtually unseen. These men ski with great grace, elasticity, and power—and in every turn and motion it was always the outside hand that led the maneuver. Even the highest-speed short swings revealed a hint of circular motion—and how else could it be? How can a skier have the forward aspect of the body and the intensely rapid action of poles in wedeln with reverse shoulder action? The bumpier the terrain, the steeper the slopes, the rougher the conditions and the closer to the fall line the skiers went, the more apparent this became."

Again, we are reminded of that German word *wendig*. This is the mark of the great skier: maneuverability, elasticity, fluidity, grace and power. And here may we say that these are exactly the qualities that the step-by-step technique proposed in this book will yield to the man or woman who has the will and the courage to become expert.

You may ask: Why, then, is reverse shoulder action so universally considered a part of wedeln? A good and a logical question which we will now attempt to answer.

A major ingredient of the answer depends on our referring to the purposeless wedeln, the so-called "mambo wedeln." This mambo wedeln has received considerably more attention (as of now) than one might suppose could be accorded a useless though pleasant maneuver. Since reverse shoulder action is part of this dance on skis, the public has come to think of wedeln and reverse shoulder action as inseparable. The reverse shoulder action, with the inside shoulder leading the turn, puts the upper part of the skier's body a half-beat behind the skis. On easy terrain this is fun and the resulting syncopation looks quite spectacular.

Let's now consider skiing from another point of view: the skier's aim in perfection of his technique and his personal feelings while skiing—one might even say the aesthetics of the art. The greatest sensation in skiing is the feeling of floating. To be light, to feel airborne, to swoop and glide—these are the exhilarating thrills of the sport. Floating turns, effortless and light (fluent and "drifted" in the sense described in our racing-car analogy) in any kind of snow or terrain, are the ultimate goal of the skier. Obviously—as we pointed out way back toward the beginning of this book—the racing skier, like the race-track jockey decked out in flamboyant silks, is more concerned with getting to the finish line than with happy, comfortable, expert movement. But (as we pointed out way back then) just as the gentleman rider hacking along a bridle path in his ratcatcher tweeds does not ride with short stirrups, his rear end up in the air and his body extended out over the neck of the horse, the recreational skier does not find himself in the distorted positions that the racing skier must occasionally assume.

Figures 108A and 108B—Comparison of Free-Form Skiing Around a Short Marker and Adaptive Position Required to Shave Close to a Slalom Pole in Comparable Position

1. Pine-bough marker.
2. Skier starts his turn around it, using normal body and shoulder motion.
3. In midturn. Note free and easy position and banking of the turn with shoulders squarely across the skis.
4. Out of the turn, relaxed and with normal, flowing forward motion.

Figure 108B

1. Skier approaches slalom gate with arms thrust forward to compensate for keeping them and the poles close to body and skis.

2. Because the pine bough has been replaced by a slalom pole which is taller than he is, his anticipation movements must be modified or adapted so that his inside arm, shoulder and pole will shave the slalom pole as closely as possible. Left shoulder, arm and ski pole must exert greater effort and be used more forcefully to compensate for immobilizing the right arm, shoulder and ski pole.

3. Extreme edging and angulation will permit skis to pass close to slalom pole while the skier squeezes by without bumping into pole (which is not a racing violation). Note the extreme difference between this picture and picture 3 in Figure 108A.

4. Although the skier has passed the slalom pole, the completion of the turn and the maintenance of equilibrium put him in this position of very extreme edging and consequent angulation to keep his body perpendicular to his skis. In this position, in a slalom race, he would be ready for attacking the next gate.

The comparison of race-track jockey and racing skier was not a random choice, as may be seen from Figure 109, wherein the normal schuss position is contrasted with the egg position used in downhill racing. The racing skier, like the jockey, eschews wind resistance and comfort in favor of speed. One of the major differences between skiing and horseback riding, however, is that despite minor variations, the fundamental dynamics of ski racing and recreational skiing are the same. Thus, in any kind of skiing, it is the entire body—elastic and in conformity—which creates the expert maneuver. Turns and maneuvers can be made with legs alone, and feet alone, and by slinging the hips from side to side. These, however, have nothing to do with the essence of fine skiing. The technique of today's superb skiers is made up of elasticity and timing. These, in turn, require rapid reflexes and a sense of lightness. There do exist strong men who can "force" a turn. This is not the kind of skiing we are talking about or the kind that is the skier's ideal. As we have repeatedly pointed out, it is not necessary to be extremely muscular in order to be a powerful skier. The power comes from technique, not from brute force.

These are not brand-new discoveries. In the thirties there was a great fad for what was then called the "jerked christiania technique." It involved reverse shoulder action and an abnormal amount of legwork. It developed hard skiing, rather than light and floating skiing. The turns were pressed and cramped, and they looked artificial rather than easy and fluent. The turns were *sideslipped* instead of being carved. Since the uphill shoulder was leading all the maneuvers, the skier had a tendency to hang on the uphill ski—which subjected him to the danger of catching the inside edges. This technique was soon abandoned in favor of more normal skiing. It was a good try and an interesting try and, like all experimentation, whether successful or unsuccessful, it helped to clarify the dynamics of skiing.

It is a wholesome and adventurous thing to have skiers constantly seeking improvements in the art and to have instructors constantly seeking improvements in the teaching of technique, with the aim of making the learning process quicker and easier. Older readers will recall, perhaps, the vogue for learning parallel skiing from the very beginning. In this system the turns were not initiated with lift to get lightness, but lightness was achieved by an abrupt forward dropping of the body which pressed the ski tips in a digging motion and robbed the sport of the wonderful floating feeling because the turns were hard and harsh rather than gliding. This instructional method had its adherents and its fans for a time. But since it proved to have more drawbacks than advantages, and since it was not suitable for deep snow or rough terrain, it was largely abandoned.

Certainly there are occasions when any maneuver which will accomplish its intended purpose is legitimate. An international racer going down a tricky slalom course will frequently be photographed with his inside shoulder leading a turn. Usually this occurs when he's

Figure 109—Normal Schuss (*left*) **and "Egg" Position** (*right*) **Compared**

1. Free and relaxed recreational schuss position, from the front . . .
2. . . . and from the side. Note closeness of skis to each other.
3. The racer's downhill stance in egg position, seen from front. It is aerodynamically desirable since it presents minimum wind resistance and affords maximum speed.
4. Egg position from the side. In this streamlined posture, the skier sacrifices fluidity of body adjustment available in normal schuss, must compensate and attain stability by keeping skis fairly wide apart, which also lines up skis, legs, arms and shoulders for minimum wind resistance, as can be seen in picture 3.

going through a hairpin combination or entering a flush or gate where he must "shave" very closely. But for recreational skiing, for fun skiing—even by champions—the occasional expedients resorted to in racing are abandoned in favor of normal, elastic, gliding skiing.

Perhaps the best final word on this controversial subject of schools of skiing is to risk repeating that we are firm believers in experimentation and healthy controversy; we believe that from these comes progress. In every technique there are virtues which have contributed to the evolution of modern skiing. For instance, the light ruáde, which Seelos introduced years ago, was adopted by the parallel technique; the leg-fanning wedeln or short swing has been incorporated into virtually every school of skiing. But these desirable additions and variations have not changed the basic principles of skiing nor do they seem likely to do so. On the other hand, it would be a sad thing indeed for skiing if ski school directors and coaches were not constantly on the lookout for possible improvements. Happily, the opposite is the case: everything new that comes along, everything that purports to be new, is closely scanned, is tried, is experimented with and debated—on the slopes and later in meetings that sometimes go on and on for hours. A rigid attitude toward ski techniques is as fatal to the interests of skiing as a rigid aspect of the body is to the skier on the slope. Change is a wonderful thing. However, we might quote the old French proverb: *Plus ça change, plus c'est la même chose.*

In any thorough discussion of schools of skiing and the dynamics of the art, there are several points that must be made for teachers and skiers alike. Some of them we've made before, but we can summarize them here in a form which the skier—having come this far—will be better able to understand than if they were in the introduction. First of all, we sincerely believe that we are not doctrinaire disciplinarians or sticklers for unnecessary procedure and detail. In fact, we maintain the exact opposite. It is our conviction (as we've stated several times in other, specific contexts) that every single step, exercise and maneuver in this book is an integral and indispensable part of the orderly and successful progression from complete novice to well-developed and all-around expert. There are ski schools and systems of skiing which offer short cuts. Some, for example, eliminate the stem turns as unnecessary. Others, honorably determined on trying to make a skier out of a beginner in a two-week vacation, have so streamlined their course of instruction that it produces skiers who are capable of exactly one maneuver, or possibly two, and who can't understand why they will never progress from that sad and boring state. The reason is clear: they lack the background to make further progress possible.

There is another thought that we must convey here, and we hope that instructors and ski-school directors will read it with care—though not all of them by far are in need of it. We refer to the tendency of some of the best-intentioned schools and instructors to forget the difference—the very real and important difference—between the completely citified beginner and themselves. Here are people who are, for the most part, natural athletes, who have spent much of their lives on skis, in the mountains, at high altitudes, in rarefied air and under robust living conditions. It is very hard for them to understand that the man who has been at a desk for fifty weeks of the year has not the physical stamina or the muscular tone to learn to ski easily and freely and with vigor and grace in the short span of two weeks.

There is also the very simple matter of respect for human weakness. For the man accustomed to steep slopes and mountain vistas, a certain amount of contempt is bound to be felt toward the city skier who is simply downright frightened of heights and slopes which are strange to him and over which he has no control. There are, it is true, people of unusual courage, and of course there are those who are rather reckless than courageous, and these are the ones who account for no few skiing accidents. But the average non-skier, or the average occasional skier, may be a person of ample courage and ample determination, and may still be completely daunted and—frankly—terrified when urged or taunted or encouraged or pushed to try to go too fast too soon. The result is an intensification of fear and a consequent tightening of muscles and an inability to relax and learn. Again, it is our belief that the graduated, systematized development of skiing technique as expounded in this book is—in the net—the shortest way and the best way (in our estimation, the *only* way) for a beginner to become an expert and to feel in himself the kind of mastery and confidence which is the source of true courage.

HOMEWARD BOUND AT DAY'S END

APPENDIXES

TOWS AND LIFTS AND HOW TO RIDE THEM

Because we know that climbing builds muscles and wind, we have not mentioned the easy way up until now, though we'd like a nickel for every reader who has turned to this chapter fairly early in the game.

Tows and lifts are extremely useful in two respects. They save the time and effort of climbing (which is of great importance to those whose skiing time is limited), and they give one a chance to rest somewhat for the next downhill run.

There is no reason why you should not use tows or lifts whenever they are available, provided you know how to climb if you have to, and provided you are in good enough condition to make the downhill run safely.

There are three main types of tows and lifts: the rope tow, the T-bar lift (double, or, when single, often called J-bar), and the chair lift. Riding them is not difficult, and observing how others do it is the best way to learn, but some pointers on the proper way to go up safely and without a spill are in order.

Rope Tows

The rope tow is an endless rope, going around two pulleys, one at the top of the hill and one at the bottom. The rope is driven by a motor, watched over by an operator who is alert to stop it if a rider falls and can't get out of the way of the next skier on his way up.

Usually, you will find packed tracks at the foot of the tow, made by other skiers. When your turn comes, get your skis into the tracks, then take off both wrist straps of your poles, and hang the poles over the wrist of the hand away from the rope. Wear your leather gloves or leather-palmed mittens even if it is a warm day. When you are set (and when you get the word from the starter, if there is one), put both hands loosely around the moving rope, and lean back a little as you gradually tighten your grip. If you don't do it gradually, the rope will jerk you off your feet.

There are two ways of grasping the rope, both satisfactory. One is with both hands in front of you. This has the disadvantage that, should the snow be high or the rope sag at any point, your poles may touch the snow and tangle with your skis. The other method is to grasp the rope in front of you with the near hand, and behind you with the hand holding the poles. If you use this second method, which has the virtue of keeping the poles behind you, use an overhand grip with the hand in front of you, and an underhand grip with the hand behind you.

However you hold the rope, once you have a firm grip on it and are riding uphill, the procedure is the same. Keep your eyes ahead, looking for unevenness, for iced or worn patches in the tracks, and for a possible fall by someone up ahead of you. Your weight should be centered squarely on your skis; if it isn't, you risk having the skis slide out from under you, either ahead of you or behind.

It is imperative, when riding a rope tow, to remember the potential danger you are in from your poles. Three things are especially important to watch: (1) Be certain to keep the tips of your poles behind you at all times, otherwise they may dig in ahead of you and jab you or spill you; (2) keep your wrist straps from becoming entangled in the tow rope, a not unlikely eventuality since two ropes have a way of twisting clockwise and counterclockwise as the tension on the spiraled hemp varies with the load; and (3) in keeping your pole tips behind you, don't trail them in such a way that one of your skis rides up on the snow rings, a sure way to fall down and an almost equally sure way to have the thongs of the ring cut or scarred by your steel edges.

If you should happen to fall, be sure to let go the rope so that you won't drag, and roll out of the way of the skier coming up behind you as quickly as you can. Don't attempt to get up and grasp the rope again; ski down or climb the rest of the way up, and better luck next time. If someone falls in front of you and is unable to get out of your way, the likelihood is that the tow operator will stop the motor. Be prepared for this. When it happens, the rope goes slack, and if you have been using it to support part of your weight, you, too, will fall. Be prepared, also, to shift your weight so as to accommodate stopping. Once you are stopped, you can hang onto the rope to keep you from sliding back, but be prepared for the tow to start up again.

While riding a rope tow, keep the elbows somewhat bent, so that the pull is against flexed muscles and not against elbow and shoulder joints, and in order to be able to "cushion" any jerking of the rope.

Don't, under any circumstances, loosen your grip on the rope in order to go more slowly. This changes the spacing of skiers on the tow, which may mean that the rider behind you will get too close for safety, and the friction of the rope going through your hands generates heat which may be sufficient to burn the palms of your gloves.

As you near the end of the tow, prepare to let go and get out of the way of the next rider. There is a level surface which is usually well packed, and as you come up onto it, release the rope and use your momentum to ski away. Here you may want to use the step turn to leave plenty of room for others and yet stay on the level. Don't stop, don't pause to get your poles gripped properly, before moving well off from the tow and the people coming up on it.

T-Bar Lifts

T-bar lifts are just what the term implies. A motor-driven cable runs high up, on pulleys mounted on towers, and from the cable hang metal bars in the shape of an upside down T if it's a double T-bar, or an L (or J) if it's a single T-bar. Whichever it is, the crossbar supports you and takes you up the hill while you hold the upright with one hand. The other hand carries both poles, again with the hand passed through the wrist straps so you won't find yourself at the top of the hill with one pole or none.

T-bar lifts always have a starter. He will tell you when to get into the tracks and show you how to stand. (There is frequently a board placed in the snow, against which you rest the tails of your skis.) As the T comes up behind you, the starter will pull it down and retard it just enough so that it comes gently against you, just below your seat. Lean back against it, but don't sit on it. As you come to rest against the T, grasp the upright firmly, with the hand nearest to it. The other hand holds the poles and keeps them away from the snow and especially away from the skis.

At the landing place, at the top of the hill, stand full on your skis and push away from the bar. Keep going until you are well out of the way.

Chair Lifts

Like the T-bar, the chair lift operates from a high cable running on towers. Chairs are suspended from it, and in these the skier sits while he rides to the top in style. Chair lifts are deservedly the most popular, since the skis are clear of the snow and the skier really rests while he rides.

Again, there is a starter who retards the motion of the chair for you, after you have got into position. The poles are held in one hand, the other hand holds the upright which supports the chair. Some chair lifts have a bar rest for the skis; usually there is none, and the skier's feet hang in the air. On such chair lifts, one must keep the tips up. All too often, a skier gazing around at the scenery, or reliving his last descent, lets his tips hang down, they catch in the snow, and he does a nose dive off his chair.

At the top of the chair lift, the snow is graded so that the skis gradually come in contact with it. At the level getting-off place, push away from your chair as you rise, a little to the side if you can manage it, and get out of the way of the next man up. If the chair is of the type that has a foot rest, it is swung out of the way just before the summit is reached.

THE SKIER'S GUIDE TO ETIQUETTE

It is not only by his faultless turns that you can recognize the fine skier, for his years with the sport have in all likelihood made the skier's etiquette second nature to him.

Your real skier is a gentleman or gentlewoman, and the first precept of his on- or off-the-slope behavior is uniform courtesy, helpfulness, and meticulous regard for the needs and comforts of others.

Before going skiing, he dresses properly and makes sure that his equipment is complete and in good shape. He knows that borrowing waxes, sweaters, bootlaces, screwdriver, or whatever else may be needed on the slope can be a nuisance to his fellows.

He will never, never keep a group making an early start waiting for him to finish his preparations. Once on the way, his equipment will be neatly strapped together, to make as compact and easily stowed a bundle as possible. On a ski train or plane he will conduct himself in the spirit of informal good-fellowship which prevails, but you will never see him drinking to excess, waxing his skis in the aisle, playing a portable radio too loudly, boasting about his prowess, pushing his way to the best seat, lolling in the diner when others are waiting.

On the slopes the good skier waits his turn at the lift, neither dawdling nor crowding the man before him in such a way that their skis may tangle. If he is climbing on skis, he keeps to the side of the trail or slope, always looking up and ahead to see what's coming. If he is climbing on foot, he does not clomp across the trail, leaving boot holes as he goes. And his skis are carried neatly and with due regard to the safety of others who might be injured or annoyed by a loosely swinging ski.

The real skier never yells "Track!" unless he has to. He uses his brakes instead of his horn.* He does not consider it amusing to swoop

---

* It may seem odd to the reader to encounter words here—where we are discussing etiquette—about the importance of controlled skiing, which has been stressed throughout the book. Yet the fact of control is an important element in the practice of ski etiquette and one that is becoming far more than merely a matter of good manners; in fact, it has assumed the proportions of an absolute essential for human safety. As slopes become more populous, as lifts develop in height and length, and as skiing fast gains popular impetus, the danger of collision becomes, increasingly, a major hazard of a sport which has otherwise become safer, thanks to the development of safety bindings and approved skiing techniques. The skier who is out of control is not only a boor and a menace to himself, he is a peril to every other skier. You can be standing perfectly still on a slope and have a skier out of control crash into you with disastrous and even fatal results for either or both of you. And bear in mind that two skiers, each traveling thirty miles an hour, making swings in opposite directions, may collide

as close as possible to beginners, in order to thrill them and scare them. If he falls, he immediately rises, fills in the hole he made, and gets out of the track of other skiers.

He does not jeopardize his safety or that of others by taking needless chances. He does not dare his less expert fellow to try a too difficult descent.

The woman skier who knows her etiquette carries her own equipment, fastens her own bindings, cleans and waxes her own skis.

No good skier endangers the limbs of his fellows by cluttering the trail with papers, garments, discarded wax containers, or anything else which might cause a bad spill and which makes the slope unsightly.

Figurative nose thumbing at the rules of a slope or at the warning of the local Ski Patrol that an area is unsafe or unready for use is not a mark of independent courage, but of childish misbehavior. Attempting a slope or trail which is marked "expert" when one is an intermediate shows one to be foolish, not brave, and a menace to other skiers as well.

If you go touring, never go alone. If, on a tour, a member of your group is hurt, never leave him alone. Send for help at once, and wait for it to arrive. The cost is loss of skiing time, a cheap price to pay for the assurance that your companion will be all right. On the other hand, ski as safely as you can, so that you will never be the cause of lost skiing time for others.

The real skier is a good companion on the way home. He keeps muddy, wet boots off the seats of cars and trains and buses; his equipment has been dried so that it does not form messy pools of water; his belongings are once more neatly assembled and stowed away.

If you are that noble creature, a punctilious skier, you also know that example to others less well trained than yourself is the best teacher for them. Help others to learn—as you yourself know, there is room and fun for all, if everyone co-operates and shows consideration.

---

with a combined impact of sixty miles an hour—enough to shatter bones and cause internal injury. So it is not only good etiquette, it is a requirement of safe recreational skiing to forego the crazy, hot-rod thrill of being out of control, to always look where you're going, and to reserve the yelling of "Track!" for those occasions (which should be rare) when emergency requires it. The skier who thinks "Track!" is an imperative directive for everyone else on the slope to keep out of his way may soon be officially banned from the slopes on which he is skiing. (We hope that time will never come, since we feel that skiing, like any other sport, is best served if it is left unregulated in so far as is possible.) It is bad enough to lose lift privileges for improper skiing, but that is as nothing compared to losing one's life or the use of one's limbs. Observing the etiquette of the slope is the best guarantee of safe and happy skiing for you and for everyone else.

CONDITIONING EXERCISES FOR SKIERS

Ski experts and physical instructors are unanimously agreed that skiing accidents are, in the large majority of instances, the direct result of poor muscular condition. This is quite apart from muscular strength. Plenty of people who are not unusually strong ski well, but they are at their best, and they are safest, when what muscle they have is in good condition.

The first requisite for safe and happy skiing is good general physical condition. Plenty of sleep, sunshine, exercise, good food, and all the other things we all know are milestones on the road to health, are fine for the skier or would-be skier. But most of us lead lives which make the taking of regular exercise, and the following of a healthy day-to-day routine, difficult to come by. And even those lucky—or persevering—few who do keep themselves in fine physical condition are not specifically conditioned to skiing.

The bane of the weekend skier is the second day on the slope, when sore muscles won't respond as they did the day before. The bane of all skiers is the first time out in a season, when the body won't respond to the orders it receives from the brain and nerve centers. The following exercises are designed especially and specifically to exercise those muscles most called upon in skiing, and to exercise them in such a way that they will be conditioned to the special stresses and strains which skiing imposes on them.

These exercises are not to be done to excess. They are time savers in that doing each one a few times will give you the equivalent exercise that doing most exercises fifty times would. However, overdoing them even a little can make you stiff and postpone your getting into shape.

It is advisable to make a chart for the week before your first ski trip of the season, listing the exercises vertically and the days of the week horizontally and checking off how many times you do each exercise. Progress will be pleasingly rapid, and seeing the results will stimulate you to keep at it. Do each exercise until you feel the muscles involved becoming quite tired, or until the breath is short—never more. After each exercise, do "the relaxer." Then write down the number of times you did the exercise and proceed to the next. A half hour should take you through the list. Do the exercises in the order shown, so that your legs, for instance, will have a respite while you do arm exercises, and vice versa. You should work up a slight perspiration toward the end of the half hour and should then have a warm bath or shower. Do the exercises barefoot, in loose clothing, outdoors or, if indoors, with open windows.

Before you start out, though, realize that we are not urging on you the drudgery of muscle building. You are preparing for skiing, not weight lifting. Exercising of the kind described here can prevent accidents because the body will be made more limber and the muscles toned. Tendons will be restored to the desired elasticity. But remember that timing and fluency are far more meaningful in skiing than mere muscle, and don't wear yourself out with exercising. (This is going to cause recriminations and unhappiness in the muscle-building ranks, but it's our advice to you.)

Finally, before you launch into a dreary regimen of self-discipline, bear in mind that skiing is fun and that preparation for it should be, too. A very good pre-skiing means for limbering and conditioning body (and spirit) is to go out dancing. Have fun and dance with all the grace and abandon you can muster. This is said in all seriousness; a good dancer can frequently learn to ski quite nicely in less than a week—whereas many muscular athletes never master skiing.

So, do the exercises as here prescribed—but take it easy! And if you can, do them to music, and rhythmically, as a skier should.

The Relaxer

To be done after each of the exercises. Stand loose and at ease. Lean against the wall with the left hand and lift the right leg slightly from the floor. Now flutter that leg, letting the foot dangle at the ankle and keeping the knee joint free and relaxed. Reverse position and flutter the left leg. Stand at ease again, then let upper body hang forward from the hips. Let it hang way down, limpy. Let the arms fall as they will, shoulders, elbows, and wrists completely relaxed. Hang the head way down, let your neck go "soft," be slack-jawed, droop the eyelids, drool, if you feel like it. The entire upper body should be utterly limp. Now, from the hips, sway from side to side, like a pendulum, very little at first, then in wider and wider arcs, remembering to stay sloppily relaxed. A minute of this will rest and refresh you.

Chair Raiser

Stand erect, facing the back of a kitchen or ladder-back chair. Grasp the uprights of the back, one in each hand, about halfway up from the seat. With stiff arms and wrists, raise chair forward and up, above shoulder height. Pause, then lower chair slowly. Start up motion again before chair legs come to rest on floor. You should be able to do this three or four times on the first try, unless you're badly out of condition, and work up to five times in three sessions. Once you can do it with some ease five times, move hands higher up from the seat when grasping the uprights, until you can hold the uprights at their extremities.

Head to Knee

Select a firm piece of furniture the top of which is several inches higher than your hip. Face it, then swing one leg up so that your heel rests on the piece of furniture. Both knees should be locked straight. Place folded hands behind head and bend forward, trying to bring the forehead against the knee of the raised leg. Help the bend by pushing the head with the hands. Push as far as you can with the count of "one," then straighten and rest for a moment, then try again to the count of "two," etc. Start the first day with two tries, lasting a few moments each, and work up to five. Few adults are limber enough to get head and knee in actual contact, but you can get closer to it by the daily five.

Push-Pull Circles

Sit erect in a straight chair, arms extended straight in front of you. Make fists. Put the right fist on top of the left fist, pushing one against the other, and then swing the locked fists in clockwise circles, making the circles as large as you can without bending either arm. As you swing your arms thus, raise them gradually, until your locked fists are describing circles over your head. Make ten clockwise circles in this way, then ten counterclockwise; then put left fist on top of the right fist and make the twenty circles again. The total of forty is your aim; if you find this exercise too tiring, start with fewer circles and work up.

Half Kick Turn Crouch

Stand with hands on hips, erect, and with the heel of one foot to the toe of the other. This is the position halfway through the kick turn. Now, keeping back straight, bend down as far as you can, hold it a moment, then rise slowly. Five of these is a good starting number. You should work up to twenty within a few days.

Wall Walking

Pace off three foot lengths from a wall, stand on the spot with your back to the wall, hands down at sides and palms facing wall. Reach back and let yourself fall back until palms touch wall, then slowly flex arms until your back touches the wall. Now push upright again, fall back again, push up again, and so on, aiming for twenty pushes as your regular daily stint. Keep the knees straight and the feet together. To vary this exercise, try "walking" up and down the wall with your hands supporting the weight of your body as above.

Chair Stand

This is by all odds the best and most basic leg exercise for skiers. Stand with your left side against the seat of a solid chair. Place the left foot solidly on the chair. Hold arms out to sides. Now, rise slowly on the left foot, keeping the right leg limber but straight. When you have risen to erect stance on your left foot, pause, then rise onto the toes of the left foot. Right foot is dangling. Hold the pose, then slowly lower again until the right foot reaches floor. Change sides and do exercise with right foot and leg doing the work. It may be necessary to start this exercise with one chair stand for each leg. Try to work up to five with each leg. You may have to make a slight take-off jump with the foot on the floor in order to get started, at first, but eliminate this as quickly as possible, since it diminishes the usefulness of the exercise.

Chair Raiser to Side

Get out that ladder-back or kitchen chair again. Stand so that its back is under your right arm. Grasp the lowest rung of the ladder in your hand and, with stiff arm, raise the chair sideways until the arm is just above horizontal. Raise the chair slowly, hold it at the horizontal for a moment, then lower it slowly. Change over and do the same with the left arm.

By now you should be ready to lie down on the bed. Do so, but don't rest; you're in position to do the "Ups." First come the leg-ups.

Leg-Ups

Lie on your back, arms flung wide, not down at your sides where the hands can help by pushing. Legs are together, extended, knees stiff, toes pointing. Now lift the legs slowly from the hips; lift until your toes are pointing to the ceiling; hold the pose a moment, then let your legs down slowly, slowly, until the feet almost touch the bed again; then up again. Do two ups to each rest. Two is good for the first go at it. You should work up to six in a week.

Body-Ups

Lie on your back, hands on thighs, legs extended. Sit up slowly, letting the head hang back until you're upright, but don't pause there. Keep going forward, reaching for your toes with your hands. When your fingertips touch your toes (or come as near as you can manage), lie down slowly again. Start with four body ups and work up to ten.

Push-Ups

Down on the floor, prone. Put the hands, palms down, on either side of your head, each hand about five inches from the head. Keeping the body rigid, neither bowed up nor sway-backed, push up until the arms are at full extension, then lower until face almost touches floor, then up again, etc. Four push-ups the first try are good. Work up to ten. If you have to let your body down to rest, give up until the next day—you've done enough for this time.

Now come two important and valuable foot exercises. They will rest you for what's still to come. The first is named after the frightening noises your feet make when you do it. Remember, each crackle you hear is doing you good!

Bone Crunchers

Stand with feet parallel, about three inches apart. Rise all the way up on your toes. Now, "roll" yourself down on the outside edges of your feet, and roll thus all the way back until you are on your heels with your toes up off the floor. Immediately, rise on your toes again and repeat. Spread the knees, so that the roll-down is really on the outside of the foot; get the toes up so high you feel the pull in your calves. Start with ten crunchers and work up to twenty.

Book Stand

Put a nice, fat telephone book on the floor, stand with your toes on it, and with your heels on the floor. Stand erect. Now, without leaning the body forward, rise onto your toes, and slowly let yourself down until your heels touch the floor, then up again, and so on for ten times. Work up to twenty.

Skier's Toe Touch

This is your old friend, touching the toes without bending the knees—with a new twist. Stand erect, reach for the ceiling, as high as you can, way, way up, head back, fingers stretching up, up, up. Now, sweep down fast and hard, getting your fingers as near to your toes as you can. Hold the position a moment, then bend the knees all the way, until you are sitting on your heels, and simultaneously extend your arms in front of you. Hold the bend while you swing your arms up, reaching for the ceiling again, and then rise slowly all the way up, up onto your toes, reaching for the ceiling—and then sweep the arms down again, trying to touch your toes. Keep it up, in rhythm, not stopping between swings. Five times is a good starter; ten times is good for anybody.

Book Lifter

Ready to lie down again? Lie supine, arms out, spread wide, a fairly heavy book in each hand. Raise the arms with elbows unbent, bringing the books together directly above your face. Lower them slowly, out to the sides again, and before your hands touch the bed, start raising the arms again. Start with five book lifts and increase to ten.

Snowplow Bends

Stand with legs quite wide apart. Turn the toes in as far as they will go. Now bend the knees toward each other and, keeping the upper body as erect as possible, strive to get both palms flat to the floor behind you. You'll never achieve it—but strive! Rise slowly and try again. Three tries the first time is enough. You should work up to doing five such bends without tiring. If you find it easy, you're starting with your legs too close together.

Bent-Arm Push-Pulls

Sit on a chair, put the fists in position as described under push-pull circles, then bend the arms until fists almost touch the chest. Now make the clockwise and counterclockwise circles again, changing top fist from right hand to left hand, and remembering to keep them pressing each other, so that one fist tries to make the circle while the other resists. Now try the same thing behind you, making the circles as large as possible. There is no "correct" number of times to do this exercise; the harder you make one arm resist the other, the more you get out of each circle.

Thigh Stretch

Stand erect, feet together and slightly toed in, arms held out at sides for balance. Support the weight on the left leg, without shifting the symmetrical body position. Now bend the left knee, at the same time extending the right leg out to the side, with knee stiff and toeing in with the foot. Bend all the way down, until you are almost sitting on your left heel, your right leg far out to the side. Now shift the weight to the right leg, at the same time bending it while the left leg straightens. When the right leg is fully flexed and the left leg is extended, rise erect again. Bring feet together and repeat the exercise, starting this time with the right leg bending. Three on each side is a good beginning. Aim for five on each side done without strain.

There is your fast daily half hour of ski conditioning exercises. Do them faithfully, and you'll ski better, more safely, and more enjoyably. Much skiing time is lost on the slopes in trying to make unwilling and unready muscles respond to the skier's needs and wishes. These exercises will prepare you to get the most out of your time and can materially accelerate the learning process.

INDEX

* *Page numbers in italics indicate illustrations.*

* *Page numbers in italics indicate illustrations.*

* Page numbers in italics indicate illustrations.

* *Page numbers in italics indicate illustrations.*

* *Page numbers in italics indicate illustrations.*